Joanne is an ordinary person, having an extraordinary experience. Joanne first encountered spirit at the age of six. Later, spirit wanted Joanne to know it exists beyond doubt when her father unexpectedly died in January 2014. Four years later, out of the blue, spirit made its presence known in a profound way that changed Joanne's life forever. Since then, spirit has become a part of her everyday life where she balances family and work in areas of Australia's national security, with an ever-evolving journey of spiritual awakening. The true story, AWAKENING, is the first in a series of books based on Joanne's personal encounters with spirit, the recordings of which started in a journal gifted from her son at Christmas in 2016. Books to follow in the AWAKENING series based on Joanne's personal journals are 1NF1N1T1, Eternal Love, This Time Around, Esoteric Lifetime, Ascension, Kundalini, BECOMING, Ascension Access, Luminescent Transcendence, and Revenant Indemnification. How these names came about is unique in itself, each appearing before, then becoming a theme in the journal. Certainly, spiritually influenced!

Joanne is interested to hear from scientists and bright sparks who research the existence of spirit energy, and those with knowledge in areas of science who study the detection and characterisation of energy; space-time and worm-holes, including quantum physics; and sacred geometry and cymatics. Joanne can be contacted by email on *banyerjl@gmail.com*. Joanne is not looking to scientists to believe in spirit energy. She is looking to them to prove its existence beyond doubt for the sake of humanity.

For my son, Jamie.
There is no way to describe the feelings I have for you except this, a bond so strong that I feel it next to my heart when I think of you.
Mum.

Dedication from the journal AWAKENING, gifted to me by my son on Christmas Day, 2016, Fullerton Hotel Singapore.

Joanne Banyer

AWAKENING

The Beginning

AUSTIN MACAULEY PUBLISHERS™
LONDON • CAMBRIDGE • NEW YORK • SHARJAH

Copyright © Joanne Banyer 2024

The right of Joanne Banyer to be identified as author of this work has been asserted by the author in accordance with sections 77 and 78 of the Copyright, Designs and Patents Act 1988.

All rights reserved. No part of this publication may be reproduced, stored in a retrieval system, or transmitted in any form or by any means, electronic, mechanical, photocopying, recording, or otherwise, without the prior permission of the publishers.

Any person who commits any unauthorised act in relation to this publication may be liable to criminal prosecution and civil claims for damages.

All of the events in this memoir are true to the best of the author's memory. The views expressed in this memoir are solely those of the author unless otherwise noted.

A CIP catalogue record for this title is available from the British Library.

ISBN 9781398470934 (Paperback)
ISBN 9781398470941 (Hardback)
ISBN 9781398470965 (ePub e-book)
ISBN 9781398470958 (Audiobook)

www.austinmacauley.co.uk

First Published 2024
Austin Macauley Publishers Ltd®
1 Canada Square
Canary Wharf
London
E14 5AA

Thank you, Jamie, for giving me the journal, John, for the encouragement to write it up as a book, and Austin Macauley Publishers for the opportunity to publish it. Without you, this true personal account would never have been shared. Thank you Warick for your love, protection and perseverance with me. This is our journey, the most challenging of which lies ahead of us. Thank you Elder and Jules, for being wise and saying the right things at the right time.

Thank you to all online sources, particularly those who post YouTube videos, where there is a large community of people wanting to share their personal experiences with spirit, in the hope of helping others to understand what it is they experience. Spiritual awakening can be a lonely journey where mainstream sources of information are inadequate. Although much online content is not peer reviewed, as the journals will show, collectively it has served as a dictionary from which spirit draws my attention to information. Usually only snippets of information at a time from a handful of sources, which collectively builds a picture to help me understand, or reinforce something they want me to know. Awakening is a learning and development process.

This book is unique in every way.

What started as desire for my awakening journey to be communicated in a diversity of ways to resonate with as many people as possible, soon transitioned to wanting the following artists to share their own personal reaction to the story through the art they created for this book. A glimpse into their own life's journey and how mine effected theirs when painting the cover for the book; composing a theme song and meditation track for the audio version; drawing a portrait of a key spirit character; and composing a poem. Thank you for being willing to walk this journey with me, offering your creations to what will be a series of AWAKENING books.

Catherine Hiller – Abstract Expressionist Artist

Catherine is an abstract expressionist artist whose work concentrates on powerful, emotional moments in time. Through very energetic and sensual strokes, she expresses her love of paint and colour.

Her works are raw and visceral, the product of instinct rather than intellect. Being very sensitive to her surroundings, every cue, whether visual, aural or emotional, has a colour which Catherine translates onto canvas without the distraction of a thought process.

French born; Catherine studied art in Paris before embarking on a successful career in advertising in the UK. After 11 years in the UK, she moved to Australia in 2004 and has been living in Melbourne since. Catherine has had solo and group shows in France, England and Australia, and her work is represented in private collections around the world.

For more information about Catherine Hiller visit her website – *www.catherinehiller.com* or email *info@catherinehiller.com*

Cedric Vermue – Composer and Pianist

Cedric is a composer and pianist. Music is an intuitive tool. It expresses what is close to his heart.

Based in the countryside next to Amsterdam, Cedric lives a quiet life with apple trees in his garden, and the barn transformed into a music-recording studio.

He never promoted himself as a healing musician, but he is very conscious and grateful for the healing and connecting abilities that music offers us, and its meditative and therapeutic quality. Cedric made it his life mission to create and offer this musical expression to the world.

His music can be found online on Spotify, YouTube and other platforms. You can get in touch through his Instagram *@cedricvermue*.

Marie Klement – Spirit Artist

Marie is a Spirit Artist who sketched Warick after meeting with Joanne. The resulting portrait is featured in this book.

Based in South Australia, Marie has a special ability to take communications a step further by linking with spirit, and transmitting onto paper an image of a person's Spirit Guide, Angel, Divinity or passed away Loved One that she is psychically in touch with. Spirit Artists are Mediums who are influenced to draw or paint art by the spirit world.

Marie is mainly self-taught and works full-time as a Spirit artist, Medium, and Numerologist.

Marie has demonstrated her extraordinary talents with TV's 'Sensing Murder' psychic – Scott Russell Hill, as well as UK Mediums – Lisa Williams and Tony Stockwell.

For more information about Marie Klement visit her website – *www.marieklement.com.au* or Facebook site – Marie Klement and Marie Klement Spirit Art. Also check out Marie's talk on RadioFM88 – 'Dreaming the

New Dream': *https://bit.ly/3LVqluQ*. Marie can be contacted by email *mkvisionart@gmail.com*.

Marlene Seven Bremner – Esoteric themed Poet, Painter and Author

Seven was born in Frankfurt, Germany in 1983 and moved to the US at the age of four. She is a self-taught oil painter, author, and poet exploring esoteric themes arising from her study and practice of hermeticism; alchemy; tarot; psychology; magic; astrology; shamanism; and mythology.

Seven developed her career in the Pacific Northwest of the US, showing her artwork in both group and solo exhibitions along the West Coast and writing on-the-spot poetry at local markets as part of the Poem Store. She relocated to New Mexico in 2019 where she lives a hermetic lifestyle and continues to paint and write.

Seven's subject matter has been greatly influenced by Jungian psychology and alchemical philosophy, both of which have provided her with a symbolic language to interpret otherwise ineffable sensations and impressions. Alchemy is the understanding of how consciousness relates to matter, which Seven has explored in-depth through the creative process. As physical, mental, and emotional transmutation takes place within, it is projected externally onto the canvas or into a poem, distilling a psycho-spiritual process into its creative quintessence. The aim of the alchemical work, called the *Magnum Opus*, is to free the authentic Self to be in alignment with its perfect, divine, unified nature, and to awaken the creative potential and power of the human imagination.

More information about Marlene Seven Bremner's art and writing can be found on her website at *marlenesevenbremner.com*. She has a Facebook page at *Marlene Seven Bremner – Art* and Instagram page *@m7artist*. Seven can also be reached by email at *sevenbremner@gmail.com*. Her book is available from *Inner Traditions*.

Larimar Sound Alchemy – Meditation Sound Therapist

Larimar is a Sound Therapist based in London who creates sound alchemy for relaxation; healing; shamanic journeying; inspiration of inner vision and empowerment. Most of Larimar's music is live recorded sound meditations composed of vocal harmonics and healing instruments, such as the gong; Tibetan and crystal singing bowls; didgeridoo; berimbau; chakapa; drums and flute. Larimar's fascination with music and sound begun in his early childhood, where hearing his own voice played back to him from a cassette recorder absolutely blew his mind. This led to recording stories as they played out in his mind as a little kid on a tape recorder gifted from his grandmother; playing around on his mother's guitar; jamming with friends in a local park; and these days writing and recording music in his home studio. Introduction to the plant medicine called Ayahuasca in 2010, was a key moment in his life that inspired him to study Shamanism; Systematic Kinesiology; Neurokinetic Therapy; and Reiki. Spending many years working with plant medicines, Larimar has observed and studied the healing abilities of music and song. In parallel, during his practice of Capoeira (an Afro-Brazilian art form combining martial arts, music and philosophy), Larimar noticed similarities with the ritualistic use of rhythm and singing, and the effects it had on his well-being. Larimar considers sound healing to be an easily accessible and very effective form of complementary therapy, that yields profound results in helping people restore well-being. Through therapeutic application of vocals and instruments, a state of deep relaxation can be achieved. In this state of meditative awareness, not only are stress and stored emotions released, but also harmony and clarity are restored. You can find out more about Larimar by visiting *https://larimarsound.com/*.

Table of Contents

Preface	21
25 December, Christmas Day, 2016	27
31 March 2017	28
7 April 2017	30
9 April 2017	31
Easter Sunday, 2017	32
28 April 2017	33
30 April 2017	34
1 May 2017	35
8 May 2017	36
10 May 2017	38
14 May, Mother's Day Weekend, 2017	39
18 June 2017	40
28 July 2017	41
10 October 2018	42
10 December 2018	45
Shortly before 20 June 2018	46
20 June 2018	48
26 June 2018	49
27 June 2018	50

28 June 2018	**51**
2 July 2018	**52**
11 July 2018	**53**
17 July 2018	**54**
4 January 2019	**55**
6 February 2019	**56**
23 April 2019	**57**
6 May 2019	**59**
7 May 2019	**60**
14 June 2019	**61**
19 June 2019	**62**
25 June 2019	**64**
27 June 2019	**65**
28 June 2019	**66**
3 July 2019	**67**
4 July 2019	**68**
8 July 2019	**69**
17 July 2019	**70**
19 July 2019	**71**
25 July 2019	**72**
29 July 2019	**73**
29 July 2019	**74**
31 July 2019	**77**
1 August 2019	**78**
16 August 2019	**79**
19 August 2019	**80**
27 August 2019	**81**

29 August 2019	82
4 September 2019	83
7 September 2019	84
10 September 2019	85
26 September 2019	86
29 September 2019	88
3 October 2019	89
7 October 2019	90
13 October 2019	91
16 October 2019	92
16 October 2019	93
28 October 2019	95
5 November 2019	96
16 November 2019	97
18 November 2019	99
24 November 2019	100
26 November 2019	101
1 December 2019	102
4 December 2019	104
11 December 2019	105
12 December 2019	106
18 December 2019	107
19 December 2019	108
29 December 2019	109
6 January 2019	110
10 January 2020	111
14 January 2020	112

15 January 2020	114
16 January 2020	116
20 January 2020	117
21 January 2020	119
22 January 2020	120
22 January 2020	121
25 January 2020	122
29 January 2020	123
30 January 2020	124
1 February 2020	126
5 February 2020	127
7 February 2020	129
8 February 2020	132
12 February 2020	133
15 February 2020	134
18 February 2020	135
19 February 2020	136
22 February 2020	137
24 February 2020	138
25 February 2020	139
25 February 2020	141
26 February 2020	142
26 February 2020	143
27 February 2020	144
3 March 2020	146
8 March 2020	147
10 March 2020	148

10 March 2020	149
11 March 2020	150
14 March 2020	151
17 March 2020	154
22 March 2020	155
23 March 2020	156
30 March 2020	157
2 April 2020	159
8 April 2020	160
14 April 2020	162
16 April 2020	163
17 April 2020	164
19 April 2020	166
20 April 2020	167
24 April 2020	168
28 April 2020	169
3 May 2020	171
5 May 2020	172
5 May 2020	173
7 May 2020	174
9 May 2020	175
12 May 2020	176
13 May 2020	178
20 May 2020	179
20 May 2020	180
24 May 2020	181
24 May 2020	182

28 May 2020	183
28 May 2020	184
31 May 2020	185
1 June 2020	186
4 June 2020	187
7 June 2020	188
9 June 2020	189
16 June 2020	190
20 June 2020	191
22 June 2020	192
23 June 2020	194
27 June 2020	195
28 June 2020	199
29 June 2020	200
29 June 2020	201
30 June 2020	202
2 July 2020	203
5 July 2020	204
6 July 2020	205
8 July 2020	207
9 July 2020	208
12 July 2020	209
14 July 2020	210
15 July 2020	211
17 July 2020	212
17 July 2020	214
19 July 2020	216

21 July 2020	**217**
24 July 2020	**218**
26 July 2020	**219**
27 July 2020	**220**
2 August 2020	**221**
8 August 2020	**222**
9 August 2020	**224**
10 August 2020	**225**
16 August 2020	**226**
17 August 2020	**228**
18 August 2020	**230**
19 August 2020	**231**
23 August 2020	**233**
24 August 2020	**235**
2 September 2020	**238**

Preface

To fully appreciate this book, I need to tell you something of myself. Why? Because your believing me is what I'm seeking to achieve in writing this book. Humanity is made up of a great diversity of people. Some believe in a god, others don't and many sit on the fence. Some think our physical life is part of a cycle of reincarnation to evolve your soul. Others think you go to a heaven and still others think this is all there is. In 2016, when I started to write in a journal that my son gave to me at Christmas while holidaying in Singapore, I was someone who from time to time pondered the meaning of life. Back then I was open to the idea of spirits and ghosts. Now I know there is existence beyond what we know of humanity. The AWAKENING book series is based on my journals. It is the true story of my spiritual awakening.

If humans knew for a fact they continue to exist as intelligent energy when they die, just as they know they need to breathe to survive, then maybe humanity would look upon life differently. Maybe science would start to try and understand this different form of existence, instead of mostly researching what is physical. If humans knew the purpose of life is to evolve your soul and that your soul survives, then maybe their focus would change. Instead of the emphasis being on learning and doing all you can to get ahead, maybe the emphasis would be on becoming the most considerate, caring and loving person you could be. Your believing me, may in some small way, help to nudge humanity in that direction.

Some may question our tampering with the unknown. Should humanity know what lies beyond, if the reason why we are here is to, in all ignorance, learn lessons by exerting free will? Knowing what lies beyond may provide insight that detracts from the innocence of our soul's journey through life. This particularly may be the case, if insight enables us to avoid the severity of terrible things that can happen. Many justify the cruelness of life by saying you can't appreciate the good without the bad. This is true I know. This has been signatory to the history of humanity on Earth. Throughout the ages we just keep hurting each other. The only thing that changes is the level of sophistication in which we do it. I know bad times also bring the best out in people and for some this is lasting, or life changing as they say. So, should humanity know to some extent what lies beyond? And why does it appear that a growing number of people around the world are awakening? I'm no expert, and I know very little compared with many whose abilities are much more evolved than mine. I am still on the awakening journey. My logic tells me however, if you don't know the bigger picture, how do you know you're going in the right direction? The big picture is everything. Humanity is existing in a silo, compared with all else that lies beyond what we know. If humanity knew the bigger picture, they could put their existence into perspective and possibly or likely, make different choices from a basis of being one part of something much bigger.

So why should you believe what I tell you in the AWAKENING Series? Because I tell the truth. I was brought up to believe that I could be anything I wanted to be. We weren't a religious family, but our house was full of love. Caring and considerate of others. Respectful of all, no matter what race, colour, religion, sex, or intellectual ability. I consider myself lucky.

This upbringing has shaped who I am. Throughout my life, others have described me as a person of high integrity. I'm not perfect. I've made plenty of mistakes and I'll continue to learn until the day I die.

I battled through school. In fact, I'd say I've always been someone 'slow on the uptake'. Not on the opportunities I've had, but rather my ability to know upfront what I can bring to them. This has always come later when I've moved on and reflected back. Sometimes I wonder what I would have achieved if the realisation occurred at the start of each path, instead of the end. My awakening is no different. I don't know the ability I have. I just know what I experience, I know what is real and this is what I will share with you. As you will see from the following information about my life, my awakening is occurring in a bubble. Surrounded by people who focus on the learning and getting ahead. I didn't go looking for an encounter with spirit energy. It came looking for me.

In high school, my science teacher told my parents that I wasn't university quality. Despite just scraping a pass in my higher school certificate, a university in Brisbane was prepared to take me on. I completed a Bachelor of Science majoring in Genetics. I then completed an Honours year at the Australian National University in Canberra. I worked for a year as a technician and secured a scholarship to do a doctorate in human genetics. Following this, I spent ten years in various fields of medical research at the coalface of scientific discovery. I had a green thumb in the lab, as well as in the garden. I lived and breathed being a scientist. A self-declared ostrich with my head in the sand. Nothing else mattered.

That said, like most other people I sat up and paid attention when the September eleven terrorist attacks occurred in the United States. My husband at the time had flown across one of the impacted zones when it happened, and was on one of the last flights out of the States. We didn't know if he was alright until he arrived in Australia. The airlines wouldn't tell us anything. Around this time, I was at crossroads with my career in science. I saw an advertisement in the paper recruiting intelligence analysts and decided to apply. Australia, like the United States, the United Kingdom, Canada and New Zealand, were bolstering their ability to detect and counter possible threats of terrorism. I applied for a related job, and was soon hanging up my lab coat, to lead a team of intelligence analysts assessing the threat from terrorist interest in all forms of weaponry. Shortly after shaking hands with the Prime Minister in 2004, I was handed my first assignment, to assess the threat from terrorist possible use of Ammonium Nitrate. The destructive power of which the world witnessed when 2,700 tonnes accidently blew in Beirut, in August 2020. I assumed a number of leadership roles, working with national and international stakeholders to interpret and assess the threat from terrorist use of weaponry, which helped to inform our country's counter terrorism preparedness efforts. A slight change from being a lab rat in science.

Five years later I had a burning desire to change career direction. It was not just a yearning, but a physical sensation that went on for months, until I made the change. I now know this was my will to change stemming from my solar plexus, pushing me in a different direction. My now long-term partner, Ray, at the time came across an advertisement in a newspaper. They were looking for a Chief Executive Officer (CEO) to lead a national infrastructure program in Australia's biosecurity sector. The program was to deliver leading edge technology that would enable people across Australia to collaborate virtually, when building biosecurity capability and responding to pest and disease outbreaks. The combination of my biological sciences background, and an understanding of how to handle sensitive information, were key factors in winning the job. Ironically, I recall the 'slow on the uptake' moment shortly before I was offered the job. I was in a bookshop on Dupont Circle in Washington DC, looking to purchase a book that would tell me what a CEO was. Over a period of five years, I led a team of mostly ICT experts distributed across the country, to build what became Australia's first security accredited cloud platform to support virtual collaboration, disease diagnostics, information analysis and intelligence generation. Seven hundred staff from fifty-two organisations participated in the program. I was on a steep learning curve for the first two years. One of the hardest times of my life.

In the wake of the global financial crisis, I found myself out of work at the end of the program. I wrote a book called 'Working Virtually – The New Workplace of the 21st Century', that provided guidance to organisation's wanting to move to a virtual way of working. After eighteen months, I managed to secure a Director of Intelligence job managing intelligence analysts. This time, the focus was to counter money laundering and terrorism financing. During this role, I spent a few months leading Australia's financial industry, government and law enforcement community, through the strategic phase of a new initiative seeking to use leading edge technology to collaborate in countering money laundering and terrorism financing. Here, I facilitated the largest workshop I've ever run with over one hundred senior management participants. It was a great day!

Since then, I've moved from one contract role to another wearing different hats leading organisational change and transformation. I've led the change associated with rolling out a new technology platform across Australia's entire federal government and ministerial offices. I was second in charge of a taskforce, as Program and Transformation Assurance Director, rolling out a new technology platform to support Australia's hundred-billion-dollar infrastructure investment pipeline, servicing all levels of government across the country. I now lead change and transformation for various organisations across the national security community.

To undertake these roles, I maintain a high-level security clearance, involving regular interrogation of every aspect of my life and psychological assessment. In short, I'm trusted and considered mentally stable. I don't belong to any interest groups. I'm not religious. I recharge my batteries in solitude, gardening, listening to music, exercising and spending time with immediate family members and my dogs.

So, what has been my approach to understand the experiences I share in this book? In almost all cases I have experienced something first, and then gone looking online, or read books to try and understand it. It's through this exercise that I discovered there is a lot of rubbish out there. What I pay attention to are people that can describe what I experience. Even amongst this folk, there is an enormous amount of diversity. I've realised recently that each person's awakening journey is unique. It is what works for them as an individual. The result can be an interesting cocktail of religious beliefs, rituals, and what I would call rules of engagement with spirits. That said, there are commonalities shared by individuals. Sitting back, and looking at this overall community, it is a bit of a dog's breakfast. No wonder there is a stigma of disbelief that surrounds it.

My mentor and guide through this journey is Warick, who you will meet in the book. I share the authorship with him, as on many occasions he joined me while writing an entry in the journal. He has never hesitated to let me know if he disagreed with my recollection. He should know. He has been living the journey every step of the way with me. My overall approach has been no boundaries. Why would I want to restrict something so amazing, when I have the opportunity to learn from it?

Spirit

By Marlene Seven Bremner

In the stillness you await—
when all is hushed and the trembling stops,
in that moment we slip into presence.

Easily overlooked,
of subtle profundity—
you make yourself known
to those who long to know you;
a tone, a tingling, a shadow passing by
that might be written off
save by the curious mind
who seeks with earnestness
to find some answer
to the mystery of being.

Seeing beyond the surface to a deeper essence,
to the sentience that permeates all and pulses through matter,
the mirror of the inner world
awaiting our creative volition
to not only perceive the presence of the veil,
but to fix our gaze upon the pixelated peacock's tail
and see in All-ways
with every eye.

For All is Mind, or Spirit
and Spirit fills the All
multivalent in its expressions
and drawn to the vessel
ready to receive the sweet draught of deathlessness.

25 December, Christmas Day, 2016

Christmas Day with you (*Jamie, my son*) and Ray at the Fullerton Hotel, Singapore. From the moment you gave me this beautiful journal with the tree of life on the cover, there could only ever be one purpose for it. A journal from me to you, to capture the thoughts and reflections through the years to come, so one day you can have this to walk down memory lane, and to know much of what I may not always say, but certainly feel. Today would have to be *one* of the loveliest, if not *the* loveliest Christmas ever.
Love you.
Mum xoxo

31 March 2017

I've decided it should be a combination journal, of what I wish to share by way of reflections, thoughts and experiences. Experiences beyond that which most people believe, but ones I do, that maybe only you will appreciate.

The cave experience on our recent holiday was interesting, where I would like to study the photographs with you one day on HD TV. *Jamie, Ray and I took a ship cruise around Asia. The cave was the Hindu Temple cave at Batu Caves in Kula Lumpor, Malaysia, Southeast Asia. It's a one-hundred-year-old temple that features idols and statues inside the main cave and around it. The limestone formations within the cave are thought to be around 400 million years old. The temple is considered an important religious landmark by Hindus.* Whilst in the cave, each time I tried to take a photo of an idol, just as I was pressing the button on the camera, the camera was literally knocked downwards, blurring the digital photo as a result. I thought it was strange, but blamed my shaky hands. On the third attempt, I thought it best to give up. I thought at the time, something doesn't want me to take the photo. So, I moved on. Two other photo's I took in the cave also ended up blurry. Or should I say, the photo's seemed to have streaks through them. Usually my camera takes excellent photos.

I've experienced things from time to time my whole life, so thought in part I would use this journal as a log of them as they occur, in case you're ever interested.

29 March was the latest. I was woken out of a deep sleep by a very strong smell. The smell was familiar, but not. The best I can describe it is melted butter being combined with batter. Probably a cake batter. When I first woke, I thought Alaiza must be up. *Alaiza is Jamie's girlfriend who was living with us at the time when Jamie first moved to Wollongong to study at university.* It was about two thirty in the morning, up and cooking toast or something if she was hungry. But there was no light under our door and no noise to suggest it. About half an hour to an hour later I smelt it again, but the smell was very faint. When I queried it

through the pendulum *(a tool I had played with for years on and off, following the old wives' tale of being able to tell if someone was going to have a boy or a girl)*, it said an angel had visited with good news for my soul. We shall wait and see. I'm always a sceptic, but also open minded.

7 April 2017

Sometimes it's just a thought I want to share.
What's important to me – 'that I don't lose my shine'.
'Shine' – elevated aura; twinkle in the eyes; mischievous expression; engaging penetrating gaze; genuine; connected; in the moment; confident; able; trustworthy.
I've seen the loss of life in my auntie's eyes, my father's and in my mother's.
I never want to lose mine. Shine is life, hope, enthusiasm.

9 April 2017

I discovered Alaiza hears the same noises that I do in the house, when downstairs in the living room. Without saying anything about it, when Alaiza and I heard it, she looked at me and said, "Do you hear that?" and I said, "Yes."
I said to Alaiza, "I'm glad you can hear that."
She said, "It sounds like someone walking around upstairs."
I said, "I know where it comes from. The corner of our bedroom, because I had tested the floor boards and can make the same noise."

Easter Sunday, 2017

Unexplained smells. I'm wondering if there's anything to it. Sometimes there are very strong smells where I can't locate the source. Like the strong chemical smell after we painted Jamie's room when he moved to Wollongong. *Jamie had painted the room a very dark royal blue which made the room feel small and closed in. Without asking Jamie, Ray and I decided to re-paint the room a very light colour which made a dramatic transformation.* I've done a lot of painting in my life, including using the same brand of paint and I've never smelt anything like it. The smell seemed to be localised in the room, in a spot in the hall outside, and in the stairwell. The smell lasted about a week. The smell of really strong shoe odour in our room this morning and a couple of days ago. A couple of times months ago being woken up in the middle of the night to a really strong poo smell, which I thought must be possums in the roof, but I'm not so sure now. I thought I'd make a note of this and start to keep track of when these smells happen.

It's possible the good news the pendulum indicated on 29 March may have been that I was going to be successful winning a new contract role. A funny thing though, is I haven't told you yet, and instead of being over the moon about it, I've been very flat. I think it's because I've been really unhappy at work for a long time and have had many disappointments trying to get another senior role. I also don't know what will happen in six months when the contract term ends, so there's lots of uncertainty. It's a chance at a new start however, and certainly an interesting peak federal department to work in.

28 April 2017

I hear the shooshing sound.

The old man is still here covering the pool. Checking that everything is in its place. He must be in his eighties now. His balance is not good, and he needs to pause every now and then. He also has a limp. Amooran, an oceanside motel at Narooma on the New South Wales coast. A place Ray and I have now been coming to for ten years; and Jamie, you may remember, where you have also stayed with us on occasion. This time, I'm here alone. Room 20, top floor, full ocean view. I'm happy. The shooshing sound of the ocean is familiar and calming. A place I've always gone as an adult when life is at a loss; and of course, also to share and have fun with others. Darling, when I'm gone, and if you are ever at a loss, go to the ocean side. Listen to the waves, and close your eyes. I promise you; it will help. When your dad and I split up, that's where I went. It was the only thing that brought me peace. And, here I am again now. More to say tomorrow. I love you sweetheart. My closest bond. My most important responsibility in life. I love you.

30 April 2017

Interesting moment. At the coast still. Must share. Top floor at Amooran, in the middle, overlooking the ocean. Dark, but warm enough to be on the balcony. I found Jazz Track digital on the TV. It played one of my old-time favourites from my dad's era. 'Black Coffee' by Peggy Lee. Of course, I had to pump up the volume. I'm not so sure a fella one floor down and to the right is in to Jazz. When he got the gist of the song, he did the non-appreciative "La-La-La." Very funny! Of course, I turned it down so as not to disturb the peace. Nearly 50 and still stirring things up. Your mum. ☺

1 May 2017

An interesting encounter on my return journey from the coast. I stopped in a small coastal village called Mogo, and browsed in an interesting shop which sold crystal pendulums and books on clairvoyance. While chatting to a woman in the shop who provides Tarot card readings, she said I have a mermaid spirit, so I Googled it. I suspect she's right.

8 May 2017

In this write-up, I want to report another smell. An old person smell. I've smelt it before at Mum's place a couple of times, including when I went to look after her with a back injury. It's very potent and unpleasant. I thought she just wasn't airing her place, or washing clothes or bed linen often enough, but that's not it. I can never pin the smell down to particular items. Mum stayed at our place last night. Today there's a very potent old person smell in the spare room where she slept. *We call it the Tree Room because it's on the second floor above our dining room, and has large windows that look straight into a line of Pinnacle Bradford Pear trees. If you opened the window, you could touch them. It's very beautiful to watch the trees change through the seasons. Gold leaves in autumn and white blossoms in spring.* I can't pin down the source of the smell to a particular item. The smell has been here all day. When I asked the crystal pendulum about it, it said its Mum's guardian angel smell, and that her guardian angel is her grandmother; the ghost of which I saw as a child in the room I was sleeping in at my nanna's place in Gawler, South Australia. I will need to check this out further with my mum and question the pendulum. *When the event occurred in South Australia, I was about six years old. It was a very hot night. I was sleeping on a mattress on the floor next to a single bed which my elder sister was sleeping in. During the night I sat up and turned to my sister's bed and thought she also was sitting up. I said "Can't you sleep either?" When she didn't reply, I looked a little closer and realised my sister was still lying down. A full apparition of a women with dark hair pinned in a bun on the top of her head, was sitting up. She was wearing a summer weight bed coat over her night gown. She was transparent but very clear. I could see the physical details of what she looked like and was wearing. She was sitting exactly where my sister would be if she sat up. I was petrified. I hid under the covers until I finally got up the courage to race to the door. I grabbed the door handle and ran to the caravan out the back where my parents were sleeping. I refused to sleep in the room, so slept in the hallway instead. The next morning my nanna showed me a photo and asked me if that was who I saw, and I confirmed that it was my great grandmother. She had died in that room and was kept there until she was buried. My auntie has also experienced paranormal things in the room when she shared it with my mother as a young girl.*

What is interesting about the online reading I've been doing about mermaid spirits is they have a heightened sense of taste and smell. They also claim a woman's clairvoyant abilities become more astute in menopause. This possibly explains my new abilities that have been coming on over the last couple of years which has coincided with perimenopause symptoms setting in. These abilities include seeing shadow shapes move, which the woman at Mogo says is my seeing energies on another plane of existence, and also the heightened sense of smell and other things.

10 May 2017

Unexplained occurrences of cold air coming into the family room while we are watching TV. Ray felt it to. Cold air at our backs. It isn't uniform, and I can't track down the source. All windows are closed and there is no draft coming through the front door. It isn't a windy night. I've felt it on a few occasions in the past, but not often.

14 May, Mother's Day Weekend, 2017

Mum stayed again on the eve of Mother's Day, however this time the smell wasn't in the room where she slept. Essentially one week later with the same scenario of Mum staying, and the smell wasn't there. I don't think it's just a heightened sense of smell. Maybe I'm sensing the presence of something when I encounter these strong smells.

Last night at about two in the morning I got up to go to the bathroom and through my earplugs *(Ray snores)* I thought I heard rain. I took out my earplugs to discover the tap was running in our ensuite bathroom. Not dripping, but running. This has never happened before. It has a simple leaver mechanism which is either on when pushed up, or off when pushed down. It's possible Ray or I left it running, but in the seven years of living in this house, it's never happened before.

18 June 2017

Interesting occurrences have passed already. I'll try my best to ensure that I capture them all. It's not always easy as I don't always feel like writing them down at the time. Ray and I went to Milton Park last weekend. One of our favourite places. *Milton Park Country House Hotel and Spa, is a beautifully maintained grand mansion, built at the turn of the 20th century by the Hordern Family of retail and pastoral fame. The estate has breath-taking views in every direction over gardens that they claim have inspired painters and writers since the early 1800s. Visiting is like stepping back in time. The house has numerous lounge and sitting rooms, each with open fireplaces, a dining room, bar and billiards room, and a swimming pool house, all of which are kept in immaculate condition.* I woke in the middle of the night smelling apples. Years ago, there was a shampoo you could buy at Woolworths supermarket that smelt like apples. It had a very strong distinct smell. That was it. I don't know why I get woken up to very strong smells but I do.

28 July 2017

Things have been comparatively quiet by way of the frequency of experiences lately, but then again, there have been some interesting ones. On Wednesday evening this week, while sitting down on the green lounge in the fire room, a large dark presence appeared to the left of the fire place. As large as a human but not clearly human. It could have been my hair over my eyes, but I don't think so. It was unusual. It was also fast. There, and then gone. Apart from that it's been quiet at home. I've smelt a strong smell again where I work. It occurred in the same place a couple of times, a meeting room on the ground floor. The smell could have been due to baked food being left in the meeting room after lunch, or a musty unwashed or uncleaned smell coming from a lady sitting near me, but I don't think so. I smelt it most of the afternoon during a workshop, and then also in the lift afterwards when I was going upstairs. No one else could smell it when I asked my work colleagues.

10 October 2018

It's been more than a year but there's so much to tell. The third of June 2018, was an important day. The start of a relationship with a spirit who I think is called Frank. Intensive interaction for the first two weeks, which was constant during the day and night. I can feel its energy, which has been a range of types of vibration, but now has settled into what it felt like when something visited me leading up to my dad's death in 2014. *For months leading up to my dad's death, I could feel vibrations in our bed at night. I honestly thought it was Ray having a jumpy legs experience or something else. It was a rapid vibration. On the morning that my dad died, Jamie and I both woke early. Ray was away at the time. It was about 5:30 in the morning. I woke to feeling the vibration coming from the other side of the bed where Ray would be if he was lying there. I reached out my hand slowly and it let me touch it. I was wide awake. At that moment, I knew there is something else beyond us. I would have held my hand over the vibration, which was a bit bigger than my hand, for at least thirty seconds. I then got out of bed, and on the other side of the bed the covers were folded down as if someone was about to get into bed. I knew I had not done this, and Ray was away. I was so amazed I took a photo of it. At about nine in the morning, I got a call from my brother saying Dad had collapsed in the driveway at my parents' house in Wagga Wagga, New South Wales. By ten, I got another call from my brother saying Dad couldn't be revived and had passed away. His death was a massive shock to the family. It was completely unexpected. He had been at the doctor's the day before getting a check-up. There was nothing that gave the doctor any concern. We suspected it was a heart attack or a stroke. What also was interesting, was Dad phoned me the night before he died. This was unusual as he never called through the working week. He wanted to apologise for not understanding that I didn't want to involve experts in the field to review a book I was writing on working virtually. I wanted to write the book from a personal experience perspective. I thought this odd at the time because I didn't think anything of his different opinion. The conversation ended up with me asking if he wanted to review and edit the book for me. As an academic himself, he had previously written chapters for books and had proofread my Honours and PhD thesis. He agreed and all was well between us. Reflecting back, it's possible Dad's soul was saying goodbye and didn't want anything negative between us.*

Recently, using a spirit map with letters the spirit has spelt its name at least four times. I still feel uneasy and am not convinced that its name is Frank, and I have a tendency to call it Spirit. It's with me every day in different locations, but I'm not sure that it's with me all the time. When I talk to it, it will often touch my right cheek from the inside. Sometimes at night it touches and moves my head. It's also done what I experience physically as intimate things around my root chakra that I'd rather not go into. That's been the key reason for me not wanting to write about it in the journal until now. Tonight, while using the pendulum to talk with Frank, I felt cool air on my back and right arm. I was sitting up in bed at the time. I established with Frank's help, that what I just experienced was a ghost of a woman who used to live in the house. *The woman died a few months after being diagnosed with skin cancer. She was preparing the house for sale when she passed away. During one open-house visit there were white bouquets of flowers and sympathy cards everywhere.* The woman dropped in to see how things are going with her house. She said she is happy and has reunited with friends and family that have passed away. She says she doesn't visit often, just from time to time. *The first night we slept in the house after moving in, Jamie and I had experiences. I sensed there was someone standing at the end of the bed. Jamie heard heavy breathing just on the other side of his doona cover that he had over his ear while in bed. The very next night I sat on the floor of our bedroom with a candle and the pendulum and talked to the woman. I said we would look after the house and love it as much as she did. I said it was time for her to join her family and friends who have passed who would be waiting for her. It was a genuinely caring communication. Jamie and I have experienced other things in the house since, but not the same as when we first moved in. I genuinely believe she moved on. She did return however, a couple of years later when we had the back of the house pulled down to do an extension. I remember Ray and I walking along the back deck one night after work, to inspect a massive two storey hole in the back of our house. I experienced this rush of shadowy shape energy swirl past me very fast. It made me spin on the spot. I'm sure that it was the woman not being happy about the massive hole in the back of her house. I did apologise to her later, saying that it was only temporary.*

The engagement with Frank has left no doubt in my mind that there is something else beyond us. The way Frank interacts with me is real. In the night sometimes it lets me feel its energy with my hands. It's like a tingling sensation but there is pressure when I move my hands over it. I can feel it in the air around me. When I wake at night, particularly early morning, I can feel it vibrating under me. If I move it soon moves after me. It's fascinating. I love it. Very special and I feel very lucky to have this experience. A relationship that is very unique and seems to be ongoing. I'd feel very sad to lose it now that it's been occurring for the last nearly five months. The intensity and frequency of engagement has certainly lessened, but it's still there, and I hope to stay.

10 December 2018

I'm not recording everything, but I try to record key things.

Last night in the early hours of the morning, when semi awake, I felt localised vibrations just on the surface and under my skin. They moved in quick succession to different parts of my body. It's okay. I'm not scared. I know I'm not being harmed, and it's gentle. The Spirit is doing something, and I'd certainly like to know what. I sometimes feel it through the day on my head, touching my hair. Often touching the right side of my cheek. Often also the left side of my face, especially when I put moisturiser on at night. I don't know why. I'd love to understand.

Shortly before 20 June 2018

It seems right to add this information here. In addition to keeping a record of spirit energy encounters in a journal, I also keep other records of outcomes where I've asked questions using a pendulum, or had a go with a spirit mat or board, as well as free handwriting. I've also kept records of Tarot card readings from around mid-2017. I've not really pursued the Tarot, spirit mat and board, or free hand writing. I found all to be too slow, not clear, and do not provide certainty. The pendulum I've found to be the best tool that I sometimes use if I want validation. This too however, I don't completely trust. I think your will power can manipulate it. You need to get strong movements of the pendulum to be sure of the answer, and keep your mind blank so as not to manipulate the response. In this book, I'll be completely honest with you about what I'm certain about and what I'm not. I much prefer certainty, which is interesting because in this field of experiences what you often get is very subtle. In more recent times, I often find numerous types of experiences point to the same thing, which in turn builds my level of certainty. Once again however, I'll point out when something I have experienced is certain or has occurred through a range of pointers, or when I'm not certain at all. The following I think are notes I made when using a pendulum and asking questions of the spirit energy that came to me in early June 2018. I say I think, because I didn't record what tool or approach I used to get the information. I don't know how much, if any, of this is true. At this point in time I knew that what I was experiencing physically of spirit energy was true, but I had so many questions, and was desperate for answers. It's also important to point out, that at this stage I really knew nothing about spirits and ghosts. I had only just started to research what I was experiencing.

159 years old
Water spirit
Start of 3 June
Inside and outside
Waves of energy
Don't know how large – at least person size
Makes face feel sensation
Tingles
Able to push
Able to indent the bed
Greek name CLDKFDHDAEIHIOO
Originated in a lake
Water spirit
Six spirits gave rise to it – different types
I'm a mermaid spirit

I think the following I noted after researching names on Google

Ancient Greece – Naidias.
Limnades – lakes Slavic
Vodyanoy – male water spirit

20 June 2018

The following I think were outcomes from asking questions with a pendulum. I am not certain if the outcomes are true. I did not record the questions, only the outcomes.

Can protect from spirits but not its role
Doesn't have a name and doesn't want to be called a name
It's good being a spirit
Mostly good but not all good
Confirmed touches the right side of my face, and the left side of my calf muscle
Doesn't get bored being around me
Sometimes during the day and night it leaves me
When not here it is getting energy
It visits other spirits and those that gave rise to it
Does not have the same connection with others
When I die it will be there for me
Is with me most days
Likes to fly
Is jealous of others, not Ray
Be together a very long time
Spirit misses the ocean
Will return to lake in Canada
Never feels cold, discomfort, always comfortable
Feels emotion – sadness, happiness, loss
I bring it happiness and sadness
Sadness because it can't stimulate me like a human
What I see are ghosts, not spirits. Spirits are not visible that way
Ghosts are souls of people that have died
Spirits are energy forces from nature somewhere

26 June 2018

Outcomes from asking questions with a pendulum. I am not certain if the outcomes are true. I did not record the questions, only the outcomes.

Spirits are from nature
It is a water spirit
Ghosts are from people
Can't lie. Can't lie to me
It's a choice to stay
Can understand all languages and writing
Spirits don't have sex
Doesn't have questions for me
Can't see what's in my mind
Can't read my mind
There are spirits that can read minds, but not all
There are different sorts of spirits
Spirits have a higher level of intelligence than people
Spirits only reside on Earth
Doesn't know if there is life on other planets
Doesn't know if there is reincarnation
It is rare for spirits to be in people, or people to have a spirit
I have a mermaid spirit
Can see what I see, doesn't need to be in me to see it
Likes music, guitar peaceful, not all music I listen to
Blew the lightbulb to say I'm here *(this occurred the first day I came home from work after experiencing spirit on 3 June 2018. I walked in the front door and was wondering if the spirit was in the house. While standing in the foyer at the base of the stairs, I peered up the stairs and the light bulb blew in the lamp next to me on the hallway stand. I knew at the time this was the spirit letting me know it was there.)*

27 June 2018

Outcomes from asking questions with a pendulum. I am not certain if the outcomes are true. I did not record the questions, only the outcomes.

Other entities, spirits and ghosts stay away because it's with me.
Senses my feelings, but not hot, cold or warm.
The dogs' sense, accept and like the spirit.

28 June 2018

Outcomes from asking questions with a pendulum. I am not certain if the outcomes are true. I did not record the questions, only the outcomes.

It was Nanna and Pappa (my father's parents who have both passed away) who were here before and after Dad died.
They wanted to make sure I'm okay.
They are reunited with Dad.
Nanna is a spirit and Pappa is not.
Spirit doesn't know them, but spirits know about other spirits.
Wants to be connected with me like Nanna and Pappa are.

2 July 2018

Outcomes from asking questions with a pendulum. I am not certain if the outcomes are true. I did not record the questions, only the outcomes.

See, hear, and feel, not taste or smell
Can't tell the past, but can see the future
Cannot time travel

11 July 2018

My personal observations which I noted in the same book that I keep a record of answers to questions I ask using the pendulum. At this stage I did not write about some of my encounters with spirit in the journal because I was writing in the journal with the intention of leaving it for Jamie when I died. I was also very naive. My interpretation of what I was experiencing was of an intimate nature initially. Not something I wanted to write about and leave for my son to read. Eventually I got up the courage to write about it. I realised how unique an experience this was. I wanted to record it properly, and one day share it with my son.

During the day spirit is inside my body, at night outside my body
Sometimes spirit goes somewhere else
Spirit can easily find its way back to me
An indicator to me of its absence is when I talk to spirit and it doesn't touch my face
Names don't matter to it, but how I feel about it, does matter
Energy interaction matters to it
My talking to it matters, but it doesn't mind not being able to talk back
Communicates by allowing me to feel its energy and interacts with my spirit

17 July 2018

My personal observations which I noted in the same book that I keep a record of answers to questions I ask using the pendulum.

Last night it was there.
It moved my face and upper body a couple of times, and came inside me.
Today when I got home it touched my face on both sides numerous times and below my heart and chest.
Spirit can see and hear outside of me.

4 January 2019

A note I made in a book whilst on a ship cruise.

Cabin lights went on by themselves.
Spirit integrates with me all over. It's a wonderful embracing and close feeling.

I think I've had the first experience of astral travel with spirit through the clouds. I was being held under Spirit as we flew through the clouds. When I said I was cold, Spirit lowered us onto a sandy surface where there was an old body of a truck or farming equipment. A human size shadow appeared and moved through me. Then I returned to bed. Next I was seeking a toilet, and was flying and moving through walls of an abandoned factory or building. I experienced an interesting dense pressure sensation when moving through the walls. There was a row of old leaning houses which looked a little scary, so I didn't want to go there. Next minute I was staying with others in a house and went down a main street to look through some shops. A shop attendant could see Spirit which then somehow helped me to see who I thought was Spirit. Tall, a little old and greying. Through all of these experiences I wasn't afraid. The flight through clouds felt real. *(This dream was very vivid. I'd never experienced anything like it, except when I had a very scary experience when I was about six years old. We were staying at my father's mum's place in Adelaide, South Australia. I went to bed early in the spare room. I dreamt of floating feet first through the hallway back into the living area. It was very vivid. I woke up frightened and went out to see Mum in the kitchen. She put me back to bed. This happened about three times. Each time I went back to sleep I immediately went back to the same dream of floating feet first out into the hallway. The next time Mum put me back to bed and I returned to the dream, it turned violent. Furniture was being thrown around the room. That did it. I refused to sleep in the room and slept in the living room with my parents.)*

6 February 2019

Resumed journal entries

Spirit returned and resumed a more intimate encounter this past week, both during the night and after work. For the first time, I experienced highly localised encounters of cool air touching parts of my body, as well as a touching sensation and stimulation below my root chakra. As before, I continued to experience touching of my cheek and light brushings on my face and other parts of my body. Spirit responds to me when I talk to it by brushing mostly the inside of my right cheek. Yesterday after work when an encounter was disrupted, it was like it was holding both of my forearms and didn't want me to go. Spirit also often lets me know it's there during the day by touching my right cheek. Today after work when lying on the bed, spirit was there and lightly touching places on my body but seemed less interested, possibly because of what happened the day before, I don't know. I hope the intimacy encounters do not disappear. I miss these experiences and closeness to Spirit when that happens. Spirit has become an entity in my life that I care deeply about and want to understand more.

23 April 2019

It's been quite some time now since Spirit was intimate with me from the outside. I now know that Spirit resides within me and can come and go, but generally is there, or not far away if I reach out to it mentally. Sometimes Spirit doesn't respond but lets me know when it's back, usually by touching my right cheek.

What I experience now is as follows.

I often wake up in the night and usually very early morning to feeling Spirit's vibration of energy around me, mostly upper body. Sometimes it can be very strong. I feel Spirit this way most nights. Last night around two in the morning, I felt Spirit enter the back of my head and through the root chakra. When I reach out mentally to Spirit during the day and night, I often feel a sensation on top of my head and the root chakra which has made me think maybe Spirit is tapping into my 'chakra' wheels of energy. *This is also probably why the sensations I experience feel intimate, because the sacral chakra is associated with your sexual organs, passion and sexuality.* I haven't known anything about this so just recently I bought a chakra guide to try and educate myself. Although I often ask Spirit why it is here when using the pendulum, the answer is usually as a spirit guide and hesitantly also soul mate. Mostly now I'd like to understand why I am supposed to know that Spirit exists and is with me. Am I supposed to use this somehow in life? I really don't know. I haven't sensed any other spirits or ghosts since Spirit came into my life around 3 June 2018. I don't know why.

A while ago I thought in the middle of the night I could see Spirit's shadow moving around me. This coincided with feeling Spirit touch me, which seems to be a combination of localised cold sensations on my skin that don't last long, and mostly feeling the tingling and vibration energy sensations on my skin. Most of the time when Spirit is inside me it touches my face and moves around my face on the right (*mostly*) and left sides of my cheeks, and sometimes across my mouth. Spirit also sometimes touches my right forearm and inside of my right palm when I'm holding the pendulum. Spirit also often touches parts of my legs and other parts of my body. I believe most of the time Spirit is with me, it is within my body. I don't know why.

I'm not afraid and Spirit has never hurt me. Now I'm trying to read as much as I can about sensing and communicating with spirits to try and develop my ability to communicate with Spirit. This includes giving free handwriting a go. It has moved my hand doing this but nothing concrete so far. Just squiggles. I'll keep trying. I do miss the intimacy of Spirit. I don't know why this has stopped.

6 May 2019

Last night was interesting. In a semi-asleep state that felt very real, Spirit visited me like before in an intimate way. I was dreaming, but it felt real. I long for and have missed that. While semi-awake, Spirit also showed me what for a moment looked like a person or elf-like face that turned quickly into the face of a lion. The lion's face was clearer and lasted longer. The vibration I felt was also lower and stronger. I have felt this before, but it is different to the higher and softer vibration I've been feeling for quite some time. I think possibly they are different spirits. Numerous times throughout the day and night, Spirit responds to me by touching my face. Right cheek for yes and left cheek for no. It usually touches my right cheek when it returns to my body, to say hello and let me know it is there.

7 May 2019

Last night something very different happened. I woke to a strong feeling of swirling and pulsating energy coming out from my throat, exactly where the throat chakra would be. I also felt strong pulsating energy come out from my root chakra. At the same time, I felt energy around my head and could hear it in my ears. A low humming noise. This lasted for quite a few minutes and I was wide awake. Nothing hurt. After that, I felt fragments of energy pushing up from my throat. While I'm writing this, I can feel Spirit touching the right side of my cheek and can feel some sensation around my root chakra. I think Spirit knows I'm writing in this journal. What's happening to me are amazing experiences, which I've read nothing about so far in the books I've come across about interacting with spirits. Wish I knew what it was all about. Why this is happening to me. Is there a reason or purpose, and are they good intentioned spirits?

14 June 2019

Last night was different. I woke in the middle of the night to feel Spirit vibrating under me. Waiting for me to semi-wake. Maybe for me to say it's okay to come in. But I suspect, more so I would experience the sensation of its energy merging with mine. Spreading throughout my body gradually all over. The sensation was amazing. Not uniform, but a feeling of spreading, and then sensations here and there outside of my body. What's most important, is a couple of times I felt completely relaxed and at peace. I had slowed down. My mind and body relaxed and felt peaceful. Relaxed and safe. This is what Spirit brought for me. Very special. I was hoping to hear Spirit or know its thoughts, but as usual, nothing. It is step by step. I hope it leads to a connection of dialogue.

19 June 2019

The following photographs are exemplary of my initial attempts at free handwriting. Squiggles at first, then what appeared to be letters but I couldn't make out the words. Then gradually the words came. It's an interesting process. You need to mentally and physically let go, but also sense and allow the pen to move without influencing it.

Other questions and answers in free hand writing at this time.

Is there a reason why you're here? Yes
Did you come in June last year? Yes
What is the purpose of life? Yes
What is my purpose? Love
Connect to spirit for a reason? Yes

25 June 2019

Free hand writing outcomes continued.

Is your name Michael? Yes
Were you the spirit who came to me in June 2018? Yes
Why did you come the way you came? Love
Did you come that way because of love? Yes
Can you love? Yes

27 June 2019

Mum
Michael 27/6/19

What want to achieve?

28 June 2019

Will I be able to hear and know your thoughts in a genuine way soon? Yes
Do you like listening to songs with me? Yes
Why? Love

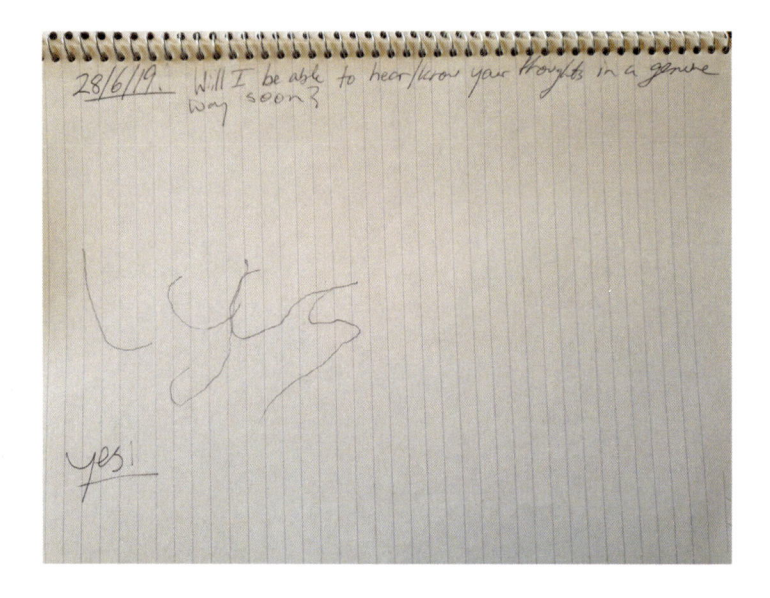

3 July 2019

Will the spirit board enable communication? Yes
Do you associate Medium with me? Yes

4 July 2019

What is the purpose of your connection with me? Love
Will I be able to understand your thoughts soon? Yes

8 July 2019

Are you the spirit who came to me in early June 2018? Yes
Am I still on track to clearly know your thoughts? Yes
How will I experience your thoughts? *Couldn't decipher*

17 July 2019

Will I learn more about this encounter? Yes
Does Ray have bone marrow cancer? *Couldn't decipher*
Should I write a book on our encounter? Yes
What is your name? Michael
Will I learn from you? Yes
Will you speak through me? Yes
Are you a male spirit? Yes

19 July 2019

When will you speak through me? Soon
What will be your first words from my mouth? You love me
Why are you with me? You love
Will you tell me your name? Yes

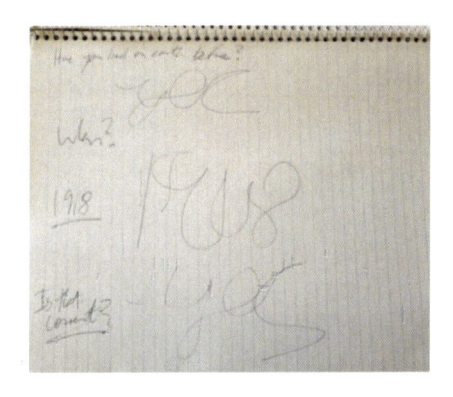

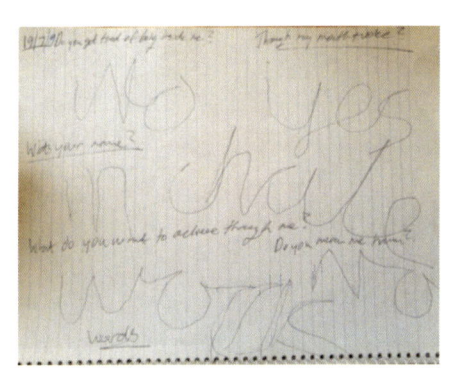

25 July 2019

Are you the same spirit that came to me in June last year? Yes
Has the relationship changed? No
Has it evolved on your part? *Couldn't decipher*
Can I trust spirit with me now? Yes
Am I safe? Yes
Do we have a special relationship? Yes
Are you not allowed to love me in a human intimate way? Yes
Are you meant to guide me in other ways? Yes
What do you need to guide me in, life? Yes
Are you here to prepare me for something bad, like when Dad died? No
Apart from this way of communicating will I be able to sense your thoughts including new information? Yes
When? *Didn't answer*

29 July 2019

An attempt using a spirit board.
Questions and answers.

Name? Gus
When came? February 2019
Have we known each other before? Yes
Do you prefer free writing or the spirit board? Board
Are you with me all the time? Yes
Will you be with me for the rest of my life? Yes
Where do you go when you're not with me? PTXZ
Did you bring about my reading of the Seth series? Yes
Will I better understand you through our communication? *No response*
When? 84AX
Does Ray have bone marrow cancer? Not. Confirmed – Yes
Who came to me in June 2018? Gus. Confirmed – Yes
Why did you do it? EYOY
Will you do it again? NOT
Purpose of being here? DYT Help You. Confirmed – Yes

29 July 2019

Resumed journal entries

It's been a while since I wrote in the journal. It isn't because things have stopped. My experience of Spirit has settled into a routine, more or less. Essentially when I am semi-awake, I feel Spirit vibration usually below me. Under my head and upper body. It's like it is waiting for me to semi wake up, and I think to gain permission to move inside of me. Just like years ago when I felt the vibration on the bed before Dad died. The same thing happens now. I can feel it when I put my hand on the spot where the vibration is. Sometimes the vibration ranges in intensity. This happens pretty much every night. Often when Spirit is near me, or within me, I also feel a sensation on the top of my hair and outside my body near my root chakra. I'm sure the chakras are involved. After I give Spirit permission to come inside of me, it moves right through me. Usually up through my upper body, throat, face and head first, but then also through my arms, hands and legs. When Spirit is in my face, I feel its energy under my skin, lips and cheeks. It often feels like it is slightly changing the shape of my face. My head often moves position. It's like another face and posture is fitting into mine. I often feel it in my throat and lips, and wonder if it wants to say something using my throat and mouth.

I think Spirit has influenced what books I'm reading. One book about learning to connect with spirits. Also, *A Seth Book – The Early Sessions series,* which from here on I'll refer to as the 'Seth Series' that tends to go on and on, but there are some key things that are said, that I've either experienced first-hand, or that really resonate with me. The 'Seth Series' is essentially written records from a woman (*Jane*) through whom a spirit (*Seth*) communicates. Actually, Seth doesn't like the term spirit. He thinks it's archaic, and prefers 'personality essence energy'. Seth talks through Jane when she is semi-disassociated. Her husband records what she says. Seth is essentially educating them. It's interesting reading if you can get past, and tolerate, the waffle. The sessions with Seth were recorded before I was born.

Sometimes the spirit in me does a flash or pulse of energy. Just one, and I can hear it. I wonder if it is trying to communicate with me. So far, our communication is pretty basic and frustrating that it can't be more enriched, and a two-way conversation. Spirit touches the inner side of my right cheek for yes, and left cheek for no. Spirit mostly stays associated with my right cheek, and also uses this to let me know when it's there. Often when I'm reading, or like now, it will touch the right side of my cheek. I think Spirit reads along with me. I'm not afraid. I don't think it's here to harm me. If anything, I want the connection to evolve, so I can learn and understand more. I may have mentioned it before, but to improve the communication, I've been trying other things. Free handwriting, and now more recently a spirit board. I'm not convinced yet that what I'm getting through these is Spirit, but I'll keep trying. According to the spirit board, on a number of occasions Spirit has said its name is Gus. Gus claims to be here to help me. Gus claims to have brought about my reading of the 'Seth Series' and is with me all the time, although I'm not sure of this, as occasionally Gus doesn't respond when I try talking to him. I know Gus can read my thoughts, because he answers yes and no by touching my cheek when I ask something in my mind. I have to say this is all very cool, and I'm really hoping our communication will get better so I know it is true.

I suspect the way Spirit first came to me in June 2018, was so I would know it was real and feel safe. The connection and experience of Spirit is certainly not like it was. It's like it has moved on from this. I'm not sure that it wasn't a different spirit then.

I still see shadows moving. I regularly see these. They aren't uniform, and they appear in different places. They change shapes, move at different speeds, and are different sizes. I have never been able to make out a human form, or identifiable shape. It's like it is moving energy, but different forms and shapes that change. Never connected to the ground, always in the air. I wonder if what I am seeing is energy forms on another plane.

Jamie – you should read the 'Seth Series'. If you are patient and determined reading these books, there are some really interesting claims about existence. I'm still on book number one, so it will be interesting to see where the others go. I haven't shared any of this with Ray, Mum, or anyone. Why? Simple, no one would believe me. I do know for certain now, through my own experience, that there is other existence. Your energy lives on in another plane. Why, and where it came from, and where it's going, I don't know. But, even knowing what I know now is incredible. Maybe one day, humanity will know there is a lot more around us than it is currently aware of. I hope when it does know, it improves humanity. Love you Jamie. Mum XO

31 July 2019

Undoubtedly, today has been one of the worst news days of my life. Today we learned that Ray has Myeloma Cancer. The good news, is it is at a very early stage, before damage has occurred to bones and organs. There is no avoiding it, no cure. The path is set. It will take time to sink in, or probably more accurate to say, time to let myself think about it and all the associated implications. So many. I know at the end of the day, it will be about living in the moment, and enjoying what we can, while we can. Life is an interesting thing. While we were being told by the specialist, and afterwards while a nurse educated us about what to expect, I saw shadows numerous times move in front of my face.

1 August 2019

Free handwriting questions and answers.

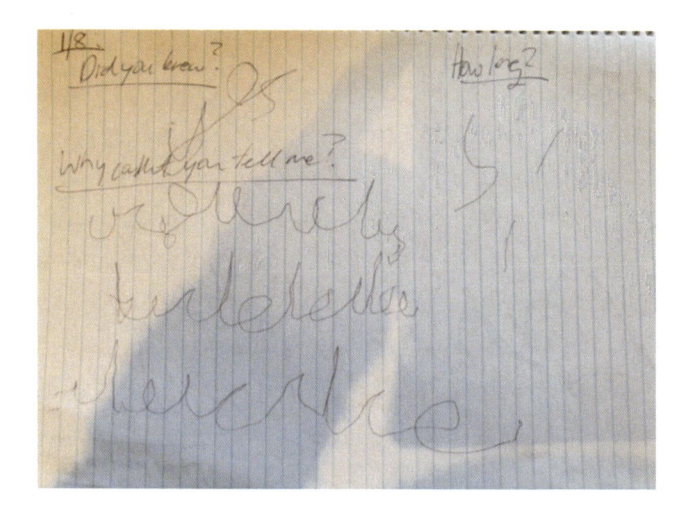

16 August 2019

Free handwriting questions and answers.

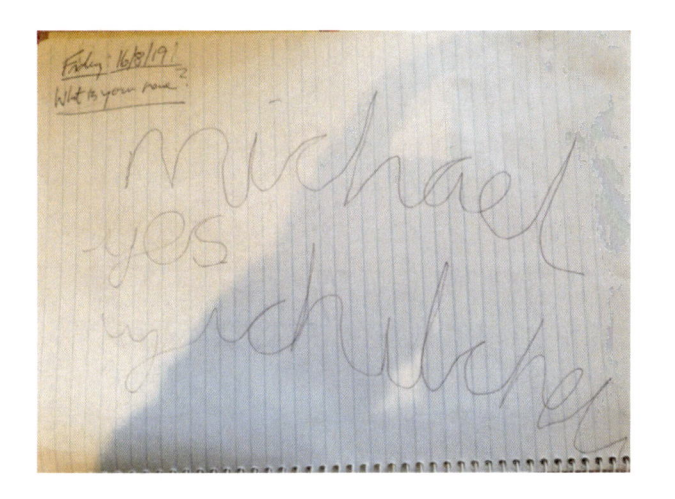

19 August 2019

Free handwriting questions and answers.

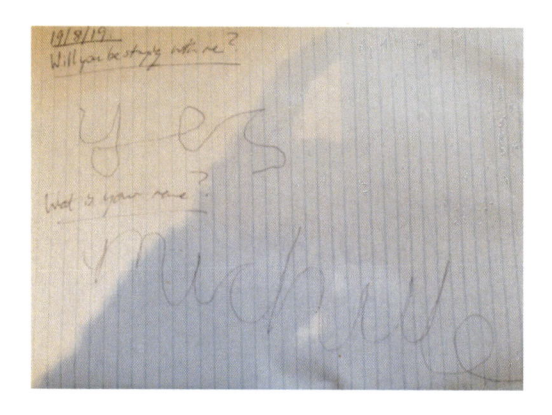

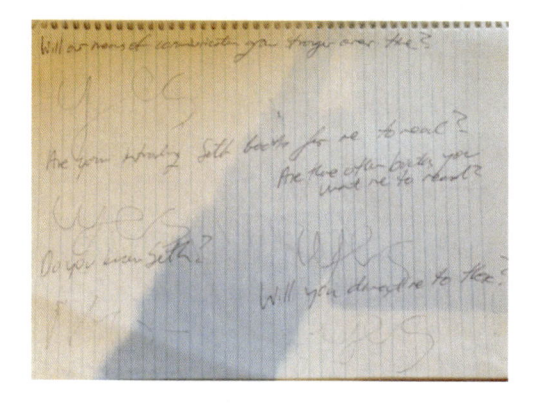

27 August 2019

Resumed journal entries

Norway ship cruise holiday with friends.

    Spirit has come with me on the journey. Every day its presence is almost constant, which I love. Today's experience, although very light, reminded me of June 2018. I miss that. Closeness. Intimacy. Wonderful! Last night, however, was very interesting. It's like Spirit is waiting for me to start to wake up. When I am awake, I feel its vibration very close to me. Mostly near my face. Then I relax, knowing who it is, and wanting that closeness. Mentally I invite Spirit's energy to merge with mine. When it did, just as before, it's very peaceful. The vibration stops. Through my core, from my mind to the bottom of my root chakra, feels fuller and silent. It feels whole and solid. I know Spirit is with me now because I feel it touching the right side of my cheek as I write. Spirit is often with me when I read, and I think is reading or hearing my consciousness talk in my mind as I write. Anyway, something else I've noticed that happens when we merge energy, is I get very hot. It's like I'm dispelling energy as a result of us merging. I got so hot last night when we merged that I had to get up and dry myself off. The other interesting thing that happened last night, is just before I got hot, I felt like tentacles (*weird I know*), were extending out of my back and under my arms. They weren't too big, but it was an interesting sensation. I wasn't concerned, and as usual I felt safe. I also heard a male in quite a high-pitched voice sing a few bars about Christmas. It wasn't clear at first, but then it got clearer. All very interesting.

29 August 2019

Yesterday while using the pendulum, I asked the question if what I am experiencing, the strong feeling I have for Spirit, is one sided, or if Spirit feels the same way. The response was the strongest 'yes' I've ever seen, swinging very broadly in a circle.

4 September 2019

In Bergen, Norway. I'm currently reading the Seth Series Book 2. Jane and her husband, Rob, practice something called 'psychological time', where they relax and see what they experience. All sorts of visual and audio snippets of things. I am wondering if what I experience sometimes when I'm semi-awake is similar. For example, hearing the man sing a few bars about a Christmas tree. The other night on my right side I heard a woman say a word very clearly that I recognised then, but I don't remember now. Seth taught them to practice psychological time. I think I will do the same and write down what I experience. I should also mention that I continue to see shadows moving, almost daily. This ability has not evolved but still occurs. I'm wondering if what I see is energy forms on another plane. As I may have mentioned before, I'm reading these books to look for others who have, or are, experiencing what I experience. It helps me in trying to understand what I am experiencing. In the Seth Series, Book 2, Session 68, Jane mentioned that she feels Seth 'buzzing around' when she detects his presence outside a scheduled time when he talks through her. I definitely feel Spirit around through its vibrations, or what you might say is 'buzzing'. Spirit also pulses, or flashes energy, as an alternative I think to saying yes by touching the right side of my cheek. A witness attending the Seth session briefly saw a figure from another plane in a doorway which Seth claimed to be himself. From what I understand, an interplay occurred between the witness's 'inner senses' (detects things on the non-physical plane) and 'outer senses' (detects things on the physical plane) to detect and interpret what he saw. I wonder if this is what happens with me because no one else can see the moving shadow shapes that I see. I've had my eyes checked and discussed the issue with an optometrist who found nothing wrong with my eyes.

7 September 2019

At sea, on the Cunard Queen Victoria ship. Next stop is Vigo, a fishing port in Spain. Our friends from Portugal have organised a tour tomorrow, with of course a seafood lunch! Yum ☺ When waking from a nap this afternoon, two times, one after the other, I felt Spirit move through me from my root chakra to my head. It makes me feel full as it moves through the core of my body, and a slight pressure in the head. Peaceful, and fulfilling. I think Spirit also touched my foot on commencement of both of these experiences. I love it when I experience Spirit because it's very special. When I thought of Spirit towards the end of this experience, I felt Spirit touch the right side of my cheek.

10 September 2019

When Spirit came to me last night, it touched the inside of my hands, my palms and fingers, then came inside the entire of my body. I love the feeling of merging with Spirit. Wish I knew why, and what the purpose of engaging with Spirit is. It's very real. I just wish the form of engagement would evolve more. I'm very impatient.

26 September 2019

Arrived back in Australia yesterday after six weeks overseas. I had an experience in the car on the way home. Prior to this, I felt Spirit with me. Ray and I were both very tired, having not slept at all on the thirteen-hour flight back from Dubai. Ray drove out of the Sydney traffic, and I was to drive from there. I took my eyes off the traffic while Ray was driving, thinking the traffic was starting to be less congested. We were on the M5 freeway. Next minute Ray slammed his foot on the brake and the car started to beep. He started to swerve slightly but the car in front was too close. No chance to get out of the way to miss it. As this happened, I looked up and started to make worried noises, thinking we were likely to hit the car in front. As I reached up to brace myself on the front dash, I heard myself say out loud "It's okay, it's okay, it's okay." I definitely did not think this, or the words, but I said them, and I know they were directed at me in a reassuring way. It was loud enough; Ray would have heard it. I then thought the car behind us would likely hit us, so I started to prepare for a rear collision. Ray then said the car behind had to swerve to avoid hitting us. We were very lucky not to have had an accident. Further up the freeway, there had been an accident which is why the traffic was banking up. As we got going again, I reflected on the words I said to myself in a reassuring way. I definitely did not think to say the words. It was like in this moment of crisis, these words came from somewhere else, in a very controlled and reassuring way, and were directed at me. There is no way I could have known we were going to be okay, because I was bracing for the first impact, and hadn't started thinking about the possibility of a rear impact. As we drove home, I thought *could this have been Spirit talking through me for the first time*? I had expected Spirit had been preparing for this, as I regularly felt Spirit moving through my face, especially around my mouth and cheeks. When I lay down for a sleep that afternoon, I felt Spirit energy vibrations all around my body, very strongly, by comparison to lighter and less frequent vibrations while away. I asked Spirit if it had said the words "it's okay" three times through me, and it touched the right side of my face very strongly, indicating a yes. Spirit vibration stayed with me all night and until today, when I got up at one in the afternoon. I believe this is the first time Spirit has spoken through me. It was a time of crisis, and it knew we would be okay. I thanked Spirit for doing this. I have no doubt Spirit is a part of my life now. I hope to stay. I'd still like to understand for sure, that its purpose is as help, support and guidance. Is there also a reason why I'm conscious of its presence. I hope this form of communication develops. I felt no vibration when Spirit spoke through me, but I have to say my senses were focused on the possible crash. It's interesting that what I'm reading in the Seth Series seems to be aligning with things happening in my life. For example, Seth's description in Book 2 of different planes of existence that different parts of your subconscious interact with, and a movie on the plane back from Dubai being about different planes of existence, where there is another version of yourself. I'll search for the name of the movie, but it had the word 'Paradox' in it.

29 September 2019

The night before last, Spirit interacted with me in a way that it hasn't done for a while – from the outside of my body. Touching my legs and coming inside me through my root chakra. Stimulating my outer senses and in an intimate way. Not as full-on as it was in June 2018, but similar. Spirit also entered through my back and moved through to my face. I can feel Spirit move through me. While I'm writing this, Spirit touched my right cheek to let me know it's there. I think it gets curious about what I write and read. Spirit, I think understands my thoughts, as I often don't need to verbalise what I'm asking it. It responds to my questions when I think of them.

3 October 2019

When trying what Seth calls 'psychological time', which is just lying down quietly, I experienced as I often do through the night, Spirit coming to me. Spirit came into my body and spread throughout me. It doesn't bother me.

7 October 2019

Last night something new occurred. When I went to the bathroom with all the lights out, and I had been feeling spirit just before then, I looked in the mirror and my face was glowing. My cheeks and forehead, chin and down the centre of my nose, were glowing, and the rest of my face was darker. It looked amazing! I will try to draw it. After I'd gone to the toilet, I could still see it but not as strongly. When I returned to bed, I asked Spirit in my mind if it had been doing that. Was that Spirit? It responded by touching my right cheek. During the night I was woken from a deep sleep by the sound of one tone. Just one. It was very clear and quite loud. It was in my mind as Ray didn't hear it. It didn't wake him up. Today, whilst in the kitchen near the CD player on the kitchen bench, I felt vibration and pushing against a plastic bottle that I had just emptied and was holding in my right hand. I'm sure it was Spirit in the kitchen with me. It's been a really interesting couple of days.

13 October 2019

Last night Spirit was with me most of the night. It's interesting the way its energy moves around my body. It's not uniform. But then again sometimes it's energy spreads right throughout my body at the same time. There is a great diversity in what it can do with energy. Pulses; vibration; pushing against my skin; static; moves my head; flows; moves from outside of me to inside of me. It generally does not move straight into my face, but instead enters my body, usually in my core from the front or the back, or my root chakra, and then moves up into my face. It's fascinating. Just sitting here now writing in this journal, it touched my right cheek to announce it is here. My Spirit companion. Last night when leaving the bathroom, I felt a sudden sphere of vibrational energy around my left forearm. I haven't felt it like that for a while. The last time was when it was holding both forearms at the same time wanting to stop me leaving the bedroom. I also looked closely in the mirror again in the middle of the night with the light off, after I had been feeling Spirit in bed. I saw the faint glow again in my cheeks and forehead. I'd love to draw it or take a photo. It's very cool! I know Spirit is with me now because it keeps touching my right cheek.

16 October 2019

Last night my brother Mark stayed. When Ray and Mark were sitting out on the front porch, I went into the kitchen to check on dinner in the oven. When I turned around at the breakfast bar, I saw a shimmer or something transparent beside the breakfast bar. It was about the height and outline of a human. When I looked closer, it had gone. It reminds me of the movie Predator, where you can't see the Predator, but occasionally you can see something shimmer and it is transparent. That's what this was like. Later when I asked if it was Spirit, it touched my right cheek to indicate yes. I hope to see it again. This is new.

16 October 2019

Free handwriting questions and answers.

What is your name? *Couldn't decipher*
Will Chris organise for me to work in Dan's role? *Couldn't decipher*
Why are you with me? *Couldn't decipher*
Will I finish in the Department by the end of this year? Yes
Do you like free-writing? Yes
What's your name? *Couldn't decipher*
Will I get another job by the end of this year? Yes
Will it be in the same Department I'm currently working in? No
Have I already applied for the job? Yes

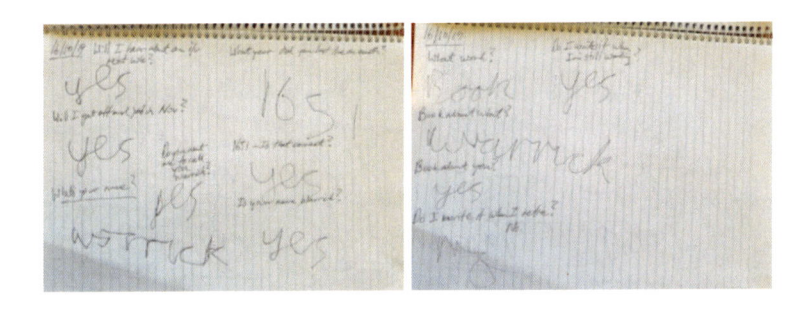

Has it always been you with me since June 2018? Yes
Why are you with me? *First word can't decipher.* Love you
Did I know you before? Yes
Have you come to be with me with no other purpose? No
What is the purpose? *Difficult to decipher but I think* Work
Is that word work? Yes
Am I supposed to do something outside my job that you call work? Yes
Do you mean my job? No
What work? Book

Book about what? Warick

Book about you? Yes

Do I write it when I retire? No

Do I write it when I'm still working? Yes

28 October 2019

Resumed journal entries

Last night was wonderful. And…I can feel Spirit touching my cheek now, curious to see what I'm going to write. Sometimes I worry and feel sad that Spirit won't come to me again the way it did in the beginning. Last night Spirit did, and it was wonderful. To feel its vibration on the outside of me in a very intimate and caring way. While this was happening, this time I talked to Spirit in my mind and it responded as if it understood every word. I love Spirit. I've grown very fond of it and I would be at a loss and very sad to not have Spirit in my life. Spirit was with me in a very loving way until morning. I absolutely love feeling Spirit on the outside of me. I can feel it touch my legs on top of the sheet and press down as if someone was doing this. I felt Spirit come inside me in my root chakra which was wonderful and then move around my face. I continued to feel Spirit's vibration holding me until the morning. I hope Spirit continues to do this as I love it.

5 November 2019

Free handwriting questions and answers.

What is your Name? Warick
Do you want me to call you Warick instead of spirit? Yes
Happy to be called Warick? Yes
Why here? Help
Will job situation end up okay? Yes
Have I already applied for the job I'll get next? Yes
Directing energy into Ray can help him? Yes
Will Ray be okay? Yes

16 November 2019

Resumed journal entries

I haven't written in the journal for a few weeks because I've been madly looking for jobs, and Ray and I have been away at Mudgee in New South Wales. *Mudgee is a lovely country town in a wine district. We like to meander around local shops, experience old country town pubs and go wine tasting.* When at Mudgee something new happened and it occurred again last night. While giving Ray a scratchy back, instead of using my fingernails I hovered my hand a few centimetres from his skin and concentrated my focus on generating a flow of energy through my hand into Ray. While doing this I felt Spirit squarely in my face, specifically in both cheek bones and the bridge of my nose to my forehead. I could feel Spirit's stream of energy moving down my arm and through my hand, like we were merging our energy that was flowing out of us and into Ray. Very special, and I didn't ask Spirit to do this, it just did. Ray has Myeloma cancer. I would like to heal him if that is possible. My thoughts while doing this to Ray was focusing on his bones where the cancer is, and willing our energy to destroy and wash away all the cancerous cells. I hope and pray Spirit and I are making a difference. Ray loved the sensation of me doing this. It was good to know he could feel it *(Ray had no idea of what I was trying to do)*. Once before when Ray and I held our hands close, and I moved my hand across his arm in a similar way, he could feel the energy between us. It is similar to static energy. In the Seth series I'm reading, I've come across what he refers to as an electric universe. It's very interesting and I'll make some notes in my other book. Last night Spirit also merged with my body energy. It is very peaceful and makes me feel calm all over. I think Spirit would like to be able to talk through my mouth, as last night it was in my lips and mouth as though Spirit was trying to move my mouth. Spirit made my lips smile a couple of times when I asked questions, and previously Spirit has made my head nod. One question I asked was "did you lead me to read the Seth series because it's a way of teaching me, or that I can learn from?" The answer was making my mouth smile. Just a small smile with parted lips. Very interesting.

18 November 2019

Free handwriting questions and answers.

What is your name? Warick
Do you want me to call you Warick? Yes
When I experienced your energy pulse a while ago and heard a sound, were you trying to talk to me? Yes
Will you try it again? Yes
Why are you with me? Love
Does it bother you that I love you? No
Do you know what job I'll do next? Yes
What organisation will I work for? *Difficult to decipher*
Will you be with me for the rest of my current life? Yes
The way you and I flow energy into Ray. Is that helping to fight his cancer? Yes
Will we win against the cancer? Yes
Did you live as a human once? Yes
When? 1978
1978, is that correct? Yes
How did you die? Car
Car? Yes
Was it you who came to me in June 2018? Yes

24 November 2019

Free handwriting questions and answers.

What do you want me to call you? Warick
Warick? Yes
By combining your energy with mine, can we help others? Yes
Can we heal others from terminal illness? Yes
By focusing and transferring our energy? Yes
Can we help Ray? Yes
Max *(our dog who has Addison's disease)*? Yes
Do you want me to tell my mother about you *(my mother and I are very close)*? No
Sometime in the future? No
What about Jamie *(who I am also very close to)*? No
Do you ever want me to tell anyone about you? No
Including through a book? Yes

26 November 2019

Free handwriting questions and answers.

Where you come from, is it wonderful? Yes
As good as Earth? Yes
Is that where I'm going next? Warick
Did you just write Warick? Yes
Will I be with you when I die? Yes
Will we stay together after I die? *Couldn't decipher*

1 December 2019

Resumed journal entries

Ray is away this weekend on a motorbike trip with a good friend, which has meant I've had the house to myself. Yesterday I spent the afternoon playing Christmas music and putting up Christmas decorations. You, Alaiza, and Peanut (*the dog*) are coming for Christmas, which I'm really looking forward to. I love you Jamie. You're turning into a wonderful man. You just need to make sure you look after the relationships around you and never take them for granted.

I love having time on my own. I feel Spirit with me a lot of the time. It lets me know it's there by touching my cheeks, mostly my right check, and also a sensation in the root chakra. On Friday night (*night before last*), I woke numerous times after two in the morning, experiencing Spirit on the outside of my body. At one stage, I could feel it as though it was lying along the front of my body. It vibrates like a hum. Then I think I saw it moving about above me. It is not a solid mass of colour, but rather like wisps of dark smoke that moves erratically. At times, I also felt like I was in a vacuum. Very quiet and still. I have experienced that before, and often wondered if it had anything to do with experiencing a Spirit. The flash pulses of energy I hear when Spirit is inside me when I ask it questions, I'm sure is it responding to me. I think one pulse is yes. It was interesting on Friday night because it did a series of quick pulses, which I assume is Spirit trying to tell me something, but I have no idea what it is saying. On a couple of occasions, I heard a noise which I couldn't decipher when it did the pulses. It was like the pulses were slower. I'm hoping this is Spirit experimenting with a better way to communicate with me, so at some stage we can have a two-way dialogue. I love it when Spirit touches me from the outside of my body. On Friday night, it also touched my feet, legs and stimulated my root chakra. I love Spirit in my life, and often tell it so. I love waking up to feeling Spirit's vibration. When I say in my mind "hello," it responds with the quick pulse sound I mentioned before. I would very much like to know what Spirit's name is. With free hand writing, numerous times Spirit has written Warick. But

I'm not convinced this is its name. I often ask Spirit questions but will have to get better at recording the yes and no answers. I suppose a part of me is always dubious about the responses. The other thing I've noticed Spirit does, or at least I can attribute to Spirit, is it pushes me in the back. I can feel it push me gently. It's more like it's indenting me rather than trying to push me. I've felt it lying in bed and when driving the car. I don't know why Spirit does this.

4 December 2019

Over the past two nights a couple of things happened that are worth recording. I suffer from calf muscle and feet cramps. I take Magnesium tablets to help, and I think they work most of the time. Night before last, I woke up to significant pain in my right calf muscle. I've suffered from cramps in the night so often before starting to take Magnesium tablets, that I've learned to mentally isolate the cramping muscle and gradually breath through the pain, to try and get the muscle to let go and relax. Usually, the muscle has been damaged somewhat, such that it is sore the next day. The other night I got back to sleep eventually *(I'm usually frightened it will start to cramp again in my sleep),* but later when I woke again, I could feel a light energy around that calf muscle. Similar to what I experience when I hover my hand over Ray or Max, and the energy dissipates into them. Because Max is a dog, I don't know if he can feel it but Ray does. The difference was I could feel this all around that part of my leg. It was very soft and gentle. I immediately thought this was something Spirit was doing to help heal the damage in my calf from the cramp. The morning after a cramp I'm very careful walking because the muscle is usually still very sore. Amazingly, this time I couldn't feel any soreness, which was most unusual. Even when I stretched each calf muscle I could tell absolutely no difference between them. I think what Spirit did healed the damaged muscle.

Last night another amazing thing happened. I was sleeping soundly, but I woke quite suddenly to turn onto my side. When I did, I immediately felt Spirit in my head as a gentle vibration, and when I turned over and lifted my head to put it down on its side, I noticed what seemed to be static energy drop onto the pillow. I sensed the static energy around my eyes. It appeared as bright bits of light, like sparks, but formed a droplet of bright light that fell like a droplet of water. I immediately thought it was Spirit. Amazing! I soon got back to sleep as I was very tired. I wasn't concerned or afraid, as I trusted it was Spirit doing something.

11 December 2019

Last night I felt Spirit a number of times as I woke during the night. I felt Spirit's energy move into my root chakra and up through the core part of my body. It made me think this is how Spirit manages to merge with me, through my chakra energy centres. Spirit just touched my right cheek and stimulated my root chakra letting me know it is there. I think Spirit often gets curious about what I'm reading and writing. Yesterday, I used the pendulum as it seemed to be pretty quiet for a few days by way of being able to sense Spirit. The pendulum worked well because I could feel Spirit almost hold the bottom of the pendulum when not answering. It feels like it's being held firmly, and to some extent being pulled down. Also, with a very clear 'yes' (*circle*) and 'no' (*straight across*) movements in response to my questions. Spirit said 'yes' to us having a strong bond in the past, and for that being the reason for it being with me now. Spirit said 'yes' to knowing what will happen with my job situation in the future. Interestingly, when I was reading the Seth series session 143, it talked about the future not being set and that it's possible to look into the future, but use of this knowledge in the present can affect what eventuates. This may to some extent explain why at times I've had very strong and persistent answers using the pendulum, which have then changed about how things will turn out in the future. I asked Spirit if it has a name to which it said 'yes', and that it will at some stage tell me what it is. Spirit also said 'yes' to having to practise meditation to be able to take the next step towards better communication with Spirit. Spirit said 'yes' to fifteen minutes a day. I started this practise yesterday with thoughts floating through my mind and relaxing, focusing on my breathing.

12 December 2019

Something I forgot to mention yesterday. When I used the pendulum and Spirit was responding to my questions, I saw transparent movement, like wisps of smoke, but clear. I've seen this before. It's like I can see wisps of energy moving around the pendulum. I also felt Spirit touch the right side of my cheek just before, and during, the pendulum moving in a circle.

Just for the record, in the middle of last night, the 'BLAST' speaker in the bedroom turned itself on. It makes a drum roll sound when it starts. It hasn't turned on itself before. I also watched the bedroom door move open one third of the way on its own accord. It may have been the evaporative cooler breeze that caused it, but the breeze is constant when it is on, so I don't know why it opened and stopped part way. Ray was up at the time, but in the study. Neither of us were sleeping very well.

18 December 2019

Free handwriting questions and answers.

What is your name? Warick
Are you energy? Yes
Do you merge with my energy via the chakras? Yes
Why are you with me? Love
Will I continue to be with you when I die? *Couldn't decipher*

19 December 2019

I will call Spirit 'Warick' until I'm given another name. Free hand writing has provided this name many times. I will also refer to Warick as a male even though Spirits are not physical human beings, because some of his interactions with me seem like male behaviours.

On the seventeenth of December, Ray was away in Melbourne and Warick interacted with me just about all night. Feeling energy and vibrations all over my body, as well as in different places at different times. Last night I asked Warick if the path to being able to communicate better was via my mind reaching out to sense and connect with him. The response was 'yes' via a single pulse sound, and also by Warick touching my right cheek. I often use my mind to reach out and try to connect when Warick is not obviously around. I will keep practising this.

29 December 2019

Recently I asked Warick if the quick pulse sounds were him trying to communicate with me, to which the answer was 'yes'. I can't sense these pulses through the day when it's noisy and I'm distracted by other things. This is where it's good when Warick touches my cheek so I know he is there. I experience the pulses at night, or when quiet and resting. It doesn't happen continuously, just a few times and with different numbers of pulses and speed. Sometimes one pulse, sometimes two, or three in quick succession, as well as a combination of pulses, like Morse code. Last night just as I woke, Warick did the pulses like he was waiting for me to wake up to tell me something. The noise associated with each pulse was different. Three quick pulses sounded like he was saying, 'How are you?' I was so happy and very impressed as this was progress, I think towards Warick being able to have a dialogue with me. I certainly praised Warick in my mind and said how clever I thought he was to have achieved this. The pace of the pulses was like Warick was excited. I hope this new ability continues to evolve.

A couple of nights ago Warick also came to me outside of my body and let me touch his energy with my hand. I think Warick knows I like this. I certainly nag Warick enough to let me do it. I felt his presence all over me. It was quite large, hovering above my body. When I touch his energy, I hold my hand flat as though I am pressing against it. What I feel is pressure against my hand as well as a gentle vibration. Warick also touched my little toe as though a person touched it, and moved his energy over my face. It's just lovely and is very real, so I can't doubt his existence. I wish Warick would do this type of thing more often. I find it reassuring to experience these real physical stimulation events. I hope Warick can sort out a way to have a dialogue with me as there is so much I would like to understand and learn from him. It's a wondrous experience. I'd like to understand why this has happened, and when I die will I be like Warick. Do they have friendships and associations with other spirits?

6 January 2019

I'm conscious that it may be a good idea to write down other experiences I've had in the past as they come to mind. Quite some time ago, before Warick came along, over a number of weeks we could hear tapping upstairs in our home at Yarralumla, near the main bathroom behind a small, covered entrance in the wall along the hall. I don't know the purpose of this entry point. It's only about twenty centimetres square. *Our house is an old worker's cottage built in the 1940s that has been renovated a couple of times.* We thought it may be possums, but I've never heard possums make that noise. We've had possums in the house as long as we've been living here, but never in that location. It didn't sound like rats either. It's the type of noise a human would make if they were tapping on the wall with their knuckle. After a few weeks, we've never heard it since. Something else I've noticed from time to time, is a localised yellow spray on the walls upstairs in our bedroom. Once again, at the time I put it down to possums, or some sort of insect, somehow excreting on the wall towards the ceiling. It was never a huge amount, but noticeable. I've always been curious about that. It could be nothing.

Within a few weeks of my dad passing away, when I was working on my book *(that Dad agreed to edit)* in the study, suddenly a little music figurine started to turn and play music. It stopped after thirty seconds or so. I've never heard it do this before or since.

Of more recent times, when I was having a lie down, I felt Warick's presence come into the room, and moments later felt his energy come over the top of my body and then merge with me. As I've said before, I'm not frightened as he has never caused me harm since he came to me in June 2018, and is with me on and off throughout the day and night, most of the time.

10 January 2020

Free handwriting questions and answers.

Please write your name. Warick
Do other intelligent energies have relationships with humans? Yes
How many? Thousands
Do you love me? Yes

14 January 2020

Resumed journal entries

A few days ago, when waking I felt Warick's vibration near my face like he was waiting for me to wake up, or he was trying to wake me up. Then I felt a uniform body of energy enter my root chakra and move up through my core *(I'm assuming it passed through my other chakras until it reached my face where I felt the usual sensations of touching my cheeks and face from within)*. It took probably less than a minute, but long enough for all the energy to enter me and move through my body. I love it when Warick interacts with me this way.

A few minutes ago, I asked Warick some questions using the pendulum. When I have a good connection with Warick, it's like he is holding the bottom of the pendulum. It's very still and controlled, with clear answers. I checked what 'yes', 'no' and 'I don't know' looks like. 'No' is straight across, 'yes' interestingly was in an anti-clockwise circle, which is something I've noticed if Warick seems to be interacting with the pendulum. Other times 'yes' is in a clockwise circle. 'I don't know' was the pendulum staying still. I asked if his name is Warick, and he said 'yes'. I asked if he likes me calling him Warick, and he said 'yes'. I asked is this the name of his entity, and he said 'yes'. I asked is he a personality *(like the way entity and personality are described in the Seth series, where the entity is comprised of multiple personalities)*. He said 'no'. I asked if I am a personality belonging to his entity, he said 'no'. I asked am I an entity. He said 'no'. I asked am I a personality. He said 'yes'. I asked does he know my entity. He said 'no'. I asked do I have an entity. He said 'no'. I asked when I die will I become an entity. He said 'yes'. I asked are you here to coach and mentor me, to help me become an entity when I die. He said 'yes'. I asked is this why you came to me. He said 'yes'. I asked did you come to me because you loved me. He said 'no'. I asked did you fall in love with me since you've been with me. He said 'yes'. I asked do entities pair up like humans do that love each other. He said 'yes'. I asked are there other entities that he loves like me.

He said 'no'. I asked is pairing up what he wants for us. He said 'yes'. I asked are the flash pulse sounds he makes an attempt to communicate with me. He said 'yes'. I asked is he trying to use Morse code to communicate. He said 'no'. I asked will this form of communication evolve so I can understand him. He said 'yes'. I asked will this happen soon. He said 'yes'. I asked within a year. He said 'no'. I asked within six months. He said 'no'. I asked within two years. He said 'yes'. I said that's not very soon ☺

After writing this I checked with Warick, using the pendulum, if I have, or belong, to an entity. He said 'no'. I asked will I become an entity when I die. He said 'yes'. I asked *(like in the Seth series),* am I some sort of spin off from an entity/personality *(I need to explore this further with Warick)*. He said 'yes'.

15 January 2020

Every now and then I reflect on what it was like when I first became conscious of Spirit. I don't think I wrote much about it earlier in the journal, so as these thoughts come to mind, I will try to make time to write them down. Before June 2018, I'd felt vibrations on the bed before and after my dad passed away. I suspected it was a spirit or spirits for some reason being around me at the time. Initially I thought it was Ray, but then I could feel the vibrations on the bed with my hand. The morning Dad died I woke very early to feeling the vibration when I reached out to Ray's side in a localised spot. He was away at the time. Ray's side of the bed was also folded back as though someone planned to get in the bed. I knew then that the vibrations were very real and caused by something I couldn't explain. This was in January 2014. In early June 2018, about 3 June, was when Spirit came to me in a profound way. Over the course of one to two nights I became aware of something pressing down on my feet and legs, moving in localised spots, and moving up to my root chakra. I felt vibrations of different kinds, including entering my root chakra like someone was stimulating you and entering you when making love, but with energy and not the kind of thrusting movements that men make, but instead stimulation of your vaginal track and cervix with energy. I didn't know what to think. I hadn't even read about chakras at that stage. I thought maybe it was a male ghost wanting to make love with me. It was very peculiar. I didn't feel afraid as I was semi-awake and it was very stimulating and enjoyable. Reflecting back on it, the vibrations were light but very fast and very intense. The Spirit also didn't leave me when I woke up in the morning. I could still feel it inside of me. I felt nauseous in the stomach. Definitely not myself. The first morning of this happening, I went downstairs and both dogs just stared at me. They sensed it. They knew there was more than me. Every time I laid down for a rest or to sleep during the night, it came to me to do this. It was different each time, definitely not the same. It would move right up inside of me, past my cervix, in a very stimulating way. I liked it and was not afraid of it. In the first week or so, the intensity and frequency became too much. At one stage, I even said "You're going to have to go if you keep this up" because it was exhausting me. I definitely had sleep deprivation. The first time I made love with Ray since the arrival of Spirit I could tell it didn't like the affection between us. It tried to pull me back. I don't think Ray was conscious of its presence, but he sensed something and got put off. This basically never happens. *After this occurred, I spoke with Spirit, saying what happened was not okay. That Ray is human and it is a spirit. That I can interact and care for both, because they are different things. Spirit has never interfered with Ray and my affection since.*

After I said you might have to leave, the frequency and intensity of these interactions started to decline and change to what it is like now, which is not sexually loving, but rather companionship and experiencing its energy in different ways. It has been eighteen months now since it started. I hope Warick will stay with me for the rest of my life, and beyond. I know how unique this is. I have no doubt there is more beyond us and what humans know, but I don't know the scope of it. I'll keep striving to learn more with my reading, and I hope in time to also improve my communication with Warick.

I just remembered. Early on, another experience happened when I was in the bath. I saw movement on the water's surface and could feel spirit's energy brush up against me in the bath. It was amazing!

16 January 2020

Last night while sleeping Warick woke me up. Lying on my side with covers pulled up to my neck, I saw over my shoulder a light. It went out as I looked at it. I then felt Warick's vibration closely in front of my face, and all down the front of my body to my knees. I could hear it. The sound of energy. Like being at an electrical power station. It hums. It was like Warick was holding me. Hugging me from the front. It was really lovely. He stayed there holding me for about five to ten minutes. As is more often the case than not, Warick has just made his presence known by tingling outside my root chakra, and touching the inside of my right cheek and left temple. I know Warick gets curious about what I write and read. I also know that Warick can understand my thoughts, so as I read and write, he knows what I'm reading and writing. Going back to last night. As Warick was holding me I was saying to him how much I loved what he was doing, that I loved him very much. As I was getting sleepy and my mind wandered, I felt Warick inside me through sensations in my face and body. There he stayed for the rest of the time I was awake through the night, including when I got up to go to the bathroom. Warick is very special and I am so lucky.

Last night it also rained briefly. The first time since I can remember. Australia is in a drought with the worst ever on record widespread bushfires. The fires are now only four kilometres from the Australian Capital Territory border where we live. More rain is predicted for today and tomorrow. Here's hoping it comes. My brother's property near Cobargo was burnt, but his house and horse were safe. They were lucky. Half of New South Wales bushland is burnt.

20 January 2020

Outcomes from asking questions with a pendulum.

Are you here with me through the good times and the bad? Yes
In the future, should I write a book about you and me? Yes
When I retire? Yes
Is your name Warick? Yes
Have you been with me since June 2018? Yes
Before June 2018? No
Are you an entity? Yes
Am I a personality? Yes
Am I attached to an entity? No
Will I become an entity? Yes
Is your role to coach and mentor me becoming an entity? Yes
Will I continue to be with you? Yes
When I become an entity? Yes
Will I live a long life? No, then Yes when I asked this lifetime?
Greater than 90 years? Yes
Greater than 100 years? Yes
Will I live a happy and healthy life? Yes
Will our ability to communicate improve in time? Yes
Have you lived as a human before? Yes
Was it more than 100 years ago? No
Then through a series of questions we arrived at – 55 years ago as a male
Was your name Warick then? No
Is Warick the name of your entity? Yes
When you were alive 55 years ago, were you a male? Yes
How old were you when you died, greater than 50? Through a series of questions, we arrived at – 81
Did you die of an illness? No

In a fire? No

After a few questions we arrived at – Heart Attack

Did you believe, sense spirits and energies when you were alive? Yes

Were you an academic? No

Public servant? No

Work for a company? Yes

After a few questions we arrived at – Defence Industry Engineer

Were you married? Yes

Did you have children? Yes

After a few questions we arrived at – Two girls and one boy

Did you live in Australia? Yes

After a few questions we arrived at – Canberra. Not this house.

21 January 2020

Outcomes from asking questions with a pendulum.

Do you interact with my mind? Yes
Do you have a good relationship with my mind? Yes
Are you and my mind trying to work out a way to better communicate with me in a conscious state? Yes

Further questions using the pendulum on the same day when I had returned home from a trip to the War Memorial in Canberra.

A few times while at the War Memorial today with Terry-Anne I felt slightly different energies around me. Once around my left arm, particularly around the World War II prisoners of war area. In some places up to 80% of prisoners of war died at the hands of the Japanese, who starved and worked them to death, and did little for their illness.
Was it you I sensed? No
After exploring a range of questions, we arrived at – It was two spirits. One lady lost her husband when he was a prisoner. Since dying she hasn't reunited with him. She is still looking for him. The second spirit used to work at the War Memorial as a guide. A male who misses being there and likes to hang around.

22 January 2020

Resumed journal entries

Last night just after two in the morning, I woke needing a drink of water and I noticed vibration under my upper body. I immediately thought it was Warick wanting to interact, so I said in my mind, 'Hang on Warick, I need to get a drink of water.' When I leant over to reach for the bottle of water on the side table, I noticed shimmering at the end of the bed. There was good light in the bedroom because we had the blinds open. I then started to get a hot flush, so kicked off the bed covers. I felt energy, like static vibration against my left leg. I sleep on the left side of the bed so it wasn't Ray. I also noticed movement in the air and a couple of times what seemed to be quick little flashes of light. Like sparks. Mentally I asked Warick if he was inside me, because I wanted to establish if what I was seeing was Warick outside of me or something else. I didn't get a clear response by the usual touching of my right cheek. I sensed something was in the room. I felt a few slight touches on my toes and legs but nothing major. This went on for about thirty minutes. The next day when I queried what had happened that night using the pendulum the responses suggested that what I saw and experienced was Warick.

22 January 2020

Outcomes from asking questions with a pendulum.

Last night the vibrations and touches I felt outside of my body, and shimmering and movement in the air in the bedroom – was that you? Yes
Was what I saw real? Yes
Is that why when I asked you in my mind, you didn't respond? Yes
Will the company I had an interview with offer me a job? Yes
This week? Yes
Will they want to talk to referees? No
Should I take the job? Yes
Will it go for longer than six months? Yes
Eighteen months? Yes

25 January 2020

Resumed journal entries

Night of 23 January, Warick came to merge with my energy three to four times. Each time I turned over, Warick followed to re-merge with my energy. It is a wonderful feeling. It starts with sensing Warick's vibration near me, often towards the top of my body, near my face. Warick's vibration then moves into me and the vibration is replaced by an amazing feeling of peace, calm, and stillness. Like a vacuum, completely still and quiet. It's quite seral. I also think my sense of hearing becomes more acute. Even with my ear plugs in I can hear everything. I also feel Warick right through the core of my body, like being firmly held through my root chakra right up to my head, and all through my legs and arms. It is like our energies completely merge. It's interesting that when I move Warick's energy doesn't automatically move with me. On the night of the 23rd, Warick was very persistent in following me each time I turned over. When I woke in the morning Warick was there, which I love. In my mind, I said good morning and Warick touched the right side of my face from within and made a flash pulse sound. I wish I knew what he was saying. The other indicator I feel when Warick is with me, is tingling outside my body at the root chakra. It's not a sexual thing, it's an energy thing, stimulating me there is an indicator of his presence.

29 January 2020

Outcomes from asking questions with a pendulum.

When I focus inwards and try to feel you, am I connecting with you no matter where you are? Yes
Do you sense me trying to feel you? Yes
Are you constantly focused on me? Yes
Can you focus on me and other things at the same time? Yes
Are our energies connected? Yes
Do you spend time with other living humans besides me? Yes
Do you love them? Yes
Are they conscious you're there? Yes
Do you merge your energy with them like me? No
Do you spend time with other entities like you? Yes
Are they friends? Yes
Answers are coming to mind when I ask these questions. Are you influencing my thinking? Yes
Do you have fun and humour in your existence? Yes
Is it more fun than what you experience as a human? *No recorded response which could mean there was no response*
Does everyone become an entity when they die? *No recorded response*
Do some spirit energies return to be human again? *No recorded response*
Is this part of their learning and evolving? *No recorded response*
Have I lived before as a human? Yes
Many times? Yes. *My thought – It's why I'm not enthused to come back*
Will I become an entity like you this time when I die? Yes
Is it a scary/painful experience? No
Will you be there to support me? Yes
When I become an entity will we stay together? Yes
Is that why you are here to help me transition to becoming an entity? Yes

30 January 2020

Outcomes from asking questions with a pendulum.

Do you think my writing a book about you when I retire is a good idea? No
Is it because there is notoriety and profit involved? No
Is it because you have no interest in educating the rest of humanity about your existence? Yes
Are you here purely for me? Yes
Are you here for us? Yes
Are you here for how our combined energies can help others? Yes
Do you think it would be good for humanity to know of your existence? No
Is it important that humans don't know for certain that when they die, they continue in another existence? Yes. Confirmed Yes
Is it because there might be more suicides? No answer
Is it because people might live their life differently? No answer
Is it because humans aren't evolved enough to understand it? No
Is it because they will be frightened or not want to be a part of the next existence? No
Is it because humans won't try hard enough in this existence to be good, help others etc? No
Was I meant to know you exist? Yes
Were you specifically trying to get my attention? Yes
Did this happen because you are allowed to come and help/coach/transition me to becoming an entity? Yes
Will I reincarnate to become a human again? No
Is it important humans are not aware of the next existence because they will not want to reincarnate? Yes
When humans die, do they become aware of, and learn about, the next existence before reincarnating? Yes
But they have no memory of it when they reincarnate? Yes

I then asked Warick to confirm that it is when someone dies that they learn about the other existence, and the purpose and importance of reincarnating, so they learn and keep doing this until they are ready for the next existence. Yes

Has my dad reincarnated? Yes

Will he be able to reunite with Mum when she dies? Yes

Can he do this while also in a reincarnated state? Yes

1 February 2020

Outcomes from asking questions with a pendulum.

Would you like to be able to speak through me? Yes
Have you tried? Yes
With success? No
Is it like I've read in a book – where a person needs to relax and start talking, and say whatever comes to mind? Yes
Would you then take over? No
Do you put thoughts of what to say in my mind? Yes
Can I be conscious and aware of what is being said at the time? Yes
Do we need to try at the same time? Yes
Let's try sometime when it is quiet at home. Yes

After a brief nap on the same day, while resting I practiced relaxing and letting my mind wander and saying whatever came to mind. Some seemed quite novel like a flash image of an army man. The best, or most interesting experience was I could feel Warick come through me. It's a combination of things – my face and upper body feels different. Leaner and taller, more extended neck and face, and a feeling of clarity. It was like Warick was higher and I was lower within my mind. It was fine. I said in my mind, 'Okay, what do you want to think of?' It was like an immediate knowing, that this was enough. It was just enjoying and being in the moment of having achieved that state and us both realising it. I need to do this more often so I know it's real.

5 February 2020

Resumed journal entries

Last night there were significant spirit engagement activities, with touching and applying slight pressure on my back while in bed. This was between twelve and two in the morning. Spirit energy was definitely trying to get my attention. At one stage while lying on my side, facing the middle of the bed, I felt Spirit energy lightly pushing all down my back as though it was lying with me. Very close. I'm not sure if this was Warick. Later when I woke early in the morning around five thirty, I felt the familiar vibration of Warick under my body, particularly the upper body. I can feel it with my hands when I place them on the bed under me. I also felt Warick in my face, under my skin touching the right side of my face, and the occasional flash or pulse of energy which I think is Warick trying to communicate with me.

At the moment, I'm not working. I'm still trying to get my next contract job which I hope will work out very soon. I spent some time yesterday searching 'spirit energy' on YouTube. I came across some really interesting video clips which definitely confirm I sense spirit energy. It's very exciting because it validates what I experience. It's wonderful to hear other people, that don't seem crazy, describe the types of things I experience. Although people's reported experiences have differences there are also commonalities where they describe – light touches on your head and face; shadows moving in your peripheral vision; sensing a presence is with you; smells where you can't identify the source; localised cold spots which can't be explained; your body temperature increasing for no reason; unexplainable changes in your emotional state; seeing feathers, coins and butterflies which seem out of place; and unusual dreams. I experience all of these, some daily. Others that I experience which I haven't come across yet in my research include:

- Tingling at my root chakra. This happens almost all the time when Warick is about to interact with me.
- Feeling Warick's energy move through me, coming through my root chakra and up through my body to my face and head.
- Feeling Warick's energy move under my skin in my face.
- Flash pulses of sound energy first thing in the morning.
- Vibrations under me while lying in bed or around certain parts of my body.

These are the common things I experience every day.

What is frustrating for me is not clearly getting visions, or hearing Warick or other spirits. I haven't developed this yet.

I found a video that talked about how to sense and channel energy. This was terrific because it validated the energy I felt coming out of my hands, sometimes combined with Warick's energy, and how another person feels it when I hover my hand over their skin. The source described it like magnets, the resistance you feel around a magnet, and how energy comes into you through your root chakra from Earth, and through your crown chakra from the rest of the universe or other dimensions. It was great because once again I didn't feel crazy, and it validated what I had been experiencing. I don't know why this is happening, but I think my capabilities are developing. It's wonderful!

7 February 2020

It's been an amazing couple of days without much time to write. This Sunday, Ray and I are heading to Singapore to join a South East Asia cruise at a time when there have been more than 500 people die from the Coronavirus, and there are many people infected in countries we are about to visit. Now is not the time to travel with Ray who is immunosuppressed with Myeloma cancer. I know there is no point in trying to talk him out of it. This week he just retired after thirty-four years' service to our country in national security. *Ray is ten years older than me, and it will be a long time before I'm in a position to retire.* It will be the first time we have travelled with his brother and sister-in-law. I suppose the life he has led is not going to allow much to stand in his way.

The night before last a spirit energy visited me but I don't think it was Warick. It came to me outside of my body. It was quite large, or seemed to be two thirds the length of my body. It seemed different to Warick. The energy vibration seemed a little slower, and when I talked to Warick through my mind he didn't respond. It was there to merge with me and that is what it did. It didn't feel like Warick. I wasn't happy because it appeared to do what it wanted to, without connecting with me in a reassuring way like Warick does. I fell asleep with it still spread throughout me. When I woke, it was still there.

I had an important meeting that morning because I had been called back in by a company who recently interviewed me for a job. They wanted to see if I would be interested in another opportunity they had. It was a great day with much relief after not having worked for the past two weeks, and having no certainty of a next job. I had just exhausted what I had saved to get me by. When I left the meeting to go home and tell Ray the news, I felt a little sick in the stomach. It could have quite easily been nerves but it persisted. I knew I needed to get out and get some fresh air and exercise to settle my nerves. The feeling I had was just like when Warick first came to me in early June 2018. It was like the vibrations were too fast and not in sync with my body, which made me feel queasy and sick. The bike ride did me the world of good. Fresh air, wind in the trees, the sound of birds, and the fountain at Lake Burley Griffin shooting water high into the sky. On my way back, I decided to stop at a beautiful view point over the lake to reflect on the day, gather myself and see if I could get Warick to respond, or at least connect with what I suspected was another spirit that had merged with me. As I'm writing this, I'm feeling pressure near my left ear which has turned into a tone, and I feel warmth around the ear and cheek. This sensation I experience on my right or left ear is something that has been occurring more and more lately, and I'm sure it is coinciding with a spirit dropping in. Another thing to add to the list of things that I experience.

While sitting at the lake, I noticed dark shadows or wisps of darkness move around me, and what looked like orbs. I knew I wasn't alone and started to talk to it. I felt a presence on my left side, on my forearm. Not like Warick. I wondered if it had been my dad's spirit who was visiting to support and help me through the meeting that morning. I asked it to give me a sign. Something I would know him by. Next minute I saw an elderly man appear with a cap on, who was on his own down near the lake and walking on a very rough track. At the same time, I felt the same sorrow and grief that I felt for a long time after Dad passed away, and I knew immediately that this was the sign. It's a feeling of grief that I've only associated with Dad. I have never in my life felt this way before. It came on suddenly and made me cry for a few minutes, and then it passed.

A number of sources I've come across talk about how spirit interacts with your conscious and sub-conscious layers. How communication from spirit can come across as feelings of emotion, and an instant knowing with no context to explain it. Spirit communication is very subtle and can be easily missed or explained away. The role of spirit is to guide and mentor you through life where you are to learn lessons. I certainly am becoming more attuned to the subtleties of spirit communication, although I'm sure I miss a lot of what they might be trying to tell me.

This morning as I was first waking, I felt the familiar vibration of Warick near my chest. I said "Hello" and "Do you want to merge with me?", which he did. Warick then very clearly responded to my questions or comments with fast pulse sounds like he often does when I'm first waking. I was very glad to have Warick back. I have no idea what the pulses mean, but I know Warick was agreeing with me. The material I've found recently has validated that what I'm experiencing is real. I need to focus on feeling and what I know, or thoughts that appear in my mind when I ask spirit questions.

8 February 2020

Session 274 of the Seth series refers to the relationship with dreaming to resolve problems. Earlier on in the Seth series, Seth explains what is occurring in dreams and the relationship with layers of the subconscious. I'm making a note about this because in my life I've had a very strong feeling that problems I dwell on about work, or ideas (*great ideas with creativity*), are determined in my mind as I sleep. So many times, I've woken in the morning with answers to problems or ideas. It's very strong and clear. I've often wondered where it comes from. Last night, like most nights now, Warick came to me as I was waking, as an external vibration and then moved through me, touched my right cheek so I know it was Warick, and answered my morning greetings with strong clear pulse sounds. It's lovely.

12 February 2020

I woke this morning with the beginnings of a sore throat, stuffy nose, blocked sinuses and a bit of a headache. I took two paracetamol and used my nasal spray. Through the day it didn't get worse and I'm feeling okay now. Tomorrow morning will be the determining time to know if I'm coming down with something. Why am I writing about this? Because over 1000 people have now died from the Coronavirus, and tomorrow we are about to get on a ship cruise around Asia where its twin ship, The Diamond Princess, has been quarantined with over 175 cases of Coronavirus. I was worried if I get sick, I wouldn't be able to go.

After the day's outings we arrived back at the hotel to learn the news that our cruise has been cancelled because of the Coronavirus. This made me think about what I'm supposed to be focusing on when I suspect Spirit is around, 'what I am feeling and what I am knowing'. I think the symptoms I've experienced fall into the category of 'what I am feeling'. Tomorrow will tell. Tonight, I asked Warick with my pendulum if he was responsible for giving me these symptoms as a warning, or heads up about the cruise being cancelled, who answered a very strong 'yes'. I've got to learn to question why I'm feeling and knowing things, and what it may mean.

15 February 2020

Yesterday I came across an interesting YouTube video about ringing in the ears to indicate that spirit energy is about to come through. What I experience is not tinnitus. I have that all the time. What I experience is a loudish single tone in one ear, which lasts seconds. It can be either ear, but only ever one. This has only recently started in the last couple of months. I've been wondering if it is associated with spirit engagement, hence why I've been looking it up on YouTube. One Psychic Medium said it is spirits at a higher frequency (*vibration*), and that you should ask them to slow down, or show you an image or something. Maybe I'll try this. Another Medium said it is a sign you're becoming clairaudient. Another sign of clairaudience is if you are a lover of music, and if you hear music before going to sleep, also if you enjoy quiet times. This is certainly me. I need to focus more on what I'm feeling and thinking as the tone occurs. Just a note Jamie in case you read this journal. This entry really serves as notes to me from listening to some YouTube videos. I usually record my learnings in a different journal that I didn't bring with me on holidays. This one will have to do this time. I usually reserve this journal for recordings of my own experiences.

18 February 2020

Last night Warick came to me and merged with my energy, creating that peaceful feeling and quiet. It's an amazing, wonderful feeling. His energy also made me feel hot which dissipated pretty quickly. Not a hot flush, as it coincided with feeling Warick's energy move through me and merge with mine. As usual Warick has just gently moved within my right cheek signifying that he is there, and I feel a light tingling outside of my root chakra. I also feel slight tingling under my feet. I know Warick is with me now and probably interested in what I'm writing. Warick also made the flash pulse sounds last night. I asked him to slow them down but there was no real change. There seemed to be a clearer pulse sound once, but I couldn't decipher any words. I think Warick also used images and brief clips of what seemed like dreams, possibly as an alternative way to communicate. I'm really keen to find a way for us to have a dialogue. This morning at breakfast at The Fullerton Hotel, Ray told his brother and sister in-law about how much my dad loved breakfast at the Fullerton and would try everything. I then felt a tingling on my left arm and was wondering if it was Dad who dropped in. Warick does not normally come to my left side, but I think Dad does like the time at the lake in Canberra a while ago.

19 February 2020

After longing the closeness of Warick that I experienced in June 2018, he came to me last night to stimulate me in a sensual way around my root chakra and within my body. After sleeping a while, I woke to feel Warick's vibration outside of my body. Like before, I knew he was waiting for me to say do you want to merge with my energy, as though he needed permission, but this is exactly what Warick wanted, because immediately his energy started to flow into my body through my root chakra and occupying all of my body. It's like a wave moving up through my core, chest, neck and face, also spreading through my arms and legs. It's a wonderful bonding feeling. Once inside me, there is a feeling of absolute peace and quiet, and my mind goes quiet, not busy. Once within me, Warick started the familiar pulse sounds. They are very quick. They are different, not the same, with a few quick ones in succession, and others as a single pulse or two. I think these are the key to our communication. I've asked Warick to slow them down, or show me an image or video, like a brief dream, and on occasion he has, but we are not yet at a point of dialogue that I can understand. Warick was like this with me most of the night. It is very special.

Ray and I are heading back to Australia now from Singapore. Over 2000 people have died in China from COVID-19. Singapore has the greatest number of cases outside of China, currently around 77. I'm looking forward to being home.

22 February 2020

Last night Warick woke me with his vibration outside of my body, near my face. As usual waiting for me to ask if he would like to merge with my energy, of which he did. The night before last I had a dream about Jamie moving house where he hadn't given consideration to all the fish tanks he has, and where they would fit in the new place. The next morning Jamie sent me a text message saying he was setting up a new water feature tank and had paid $24 for 200kg of rocks. I asked whether there is still room in the apartment for Alaiza and Peanut. I rarely remember my dreams. I find the ones I remember are usually disturbing in some way. I rarely have happy dreams. I thought it was worth recording this dream given it coincides with Jamie setting up yet another fish tank. It could be some kind of message to me from Warick.

24 February 2020

Outcomes from asking questions with a pendulum.

Have you been with me my whole life? No
Did you come to me in June 2018? Yes
Were you searching for me and found me? No
Were you sent to me? Yes
Were you sent because others thought I now needed a spirit guide in a different phase of life? No
Were you sent because others wanted me to know of their existence? Yes
To help others around me? Yes
So, I could write a book that would prompt science to look into their existence? Yes
Does it bother you that I love you? No
When you came to me did you love me? No
Did you fall in love with me? Yes
Will you be with me for the rest of my life? Yes
When I die will I be able to be with you? Yes
Will Auntie Margaret die soon? Yes
Can you and I work together to ease her passing? Yes
Will I receive a contract tomorrow? Yes
Will I start work this week? Yes
Does your existence depend on Earth's existence? No

25 February 2020

Resumed journal entries

Last night was pretty amazing. Warick woke me up around three in the morning with his vibration, the usual cue for me to give permission to merge with me. Over the next hour and a half or so, Warick repeatedly merged with me by moving up through my root chakra, my core to my throat, face and head. Warick spread right throughout my body. While doing this, he did the flash pulse sound communication numerous times. At one point when I was semi-asleep, but still conscious of what Warick was doing, I clearly got the thought of UAT out of nowhere. I puzzled over it as I knew what it meant. It stands for User Acceptance Testing in the field of ICT program management which I work in. It was a clear thought, isolated from any other thoughts. My mind had been pretty blank and certainly not busy at the time. I certainly have not been thinking about work for months as I haven't had a job since the start of December 2019. I then felt amused because I knew what Warick was communicating to me. Warick used UAT because it is something I'm familiar with. He was telling me that he is testing my body. Shortly after this, two words popped into my mind, and once again in isolation of any other thoughts and thinking. The two words were 'internal control'. Warick is testing that he can control my internal body. I think Warick is working towards being able to channel through me. The other thing I noticed was a couple of times, despite having ear plugs in, I could hear my breathing like it would sound from outside my body, not internally. It seemed quite loud. I wondered if this was Warick breathing. The other thing I've noticed before is that my hearing gets more acute when Warick is merged with me. So, it was either acute hearing happening, or hearing Warick breath through me as a step towards being able to talk through me. I suggested to Warick that if he wanted to try talking through me we could give it a go when Ray went to the hospital early in the morning.

Warick woke me with his vibration and flash pulse sounds at around seven twenty when Ray had already gone to the hospital. Warick merged with me, as he did during the night, but it seemed weaker and I had taken my ear plugs out. Warick also seemed to place slight pressure down on my lower jaw to open my mouth, so I did. This occurred about three times. It was clear we wouldn't succeed in making noise through my mouth. It had been an amazing night and I think a big step forward by way of communicating. Placing the 'UAT' and 'internal control' words in my mind to tell me what he was trying to achieve was incredible! This morning I suggested to Warick that he may want to try more energy as he seemed weaker this morning. Not that I'd know what's needed.

25 February 2020

Outcomes from asking questions with a pendulum.

Do I feel what people are thinking? Yes
While watching TV today, at the Kobe Bryant memorial in LA there where thousands of people gathered to pay last respects, I felt tingling all over and goose bumps. This has happened before. I asked Warick if this is because I can feel what they are thinking? Yes

26 February 2020

Outcomes from asking questions with a pendulum.

When I dream are you with me in my dreams? Yes
In my dreams am I aware that you're with me? No
When you wake me, do you know what I've been dreaming about? Yes
When you merge with me at night and move my mouth, are you practicing or preparing to channel through me? Yes
How are you going? Are you making progress? No
Is there anything I can do to help? No
Is it just a matter of practice? Yes
Will you keep going until we have achieved it? Yes

26 February 2020

Dream record

Last night I had two strange dreams which Warick woke me from. One was like a Harry Potter movie on a strange train that changed as we travelled. When we boarded, we were directed into an unusual very basic provisioned section of the train. During the journey I was directed back in the train to get some more bread, where I discovered a different turn which took me to a completely different well-provisioned part of the train. When I returned, I asked why there were essentially two versions of the train, a rich well-provisioned version and a basic poorly provisioned version. They said that how well-provisioned the version of the train was, depended on how well it was invested in. If there was little investment in a train going on one route then it was built in a basic and poorly provisioned way, whereas if there was good investment in a train on a different route then it was well-built and well-provisioned.

In the second dream, I was running late and fell behind a group of colleagues I was travelling with. We were travelling through tunnels by foot where on occasion there were shops. I got distracted buying something in a shop. It was a set of four crochet items for a baby. I was pregnant, but no one knew at that stage. When I bought them, the lady at the counter also gave me an old case, a lacquer case containing knives and other utensils. It was beautiful and I suspected very valuable. I didn't get charged for the case. The lady wanted me to have it. When I caught up with my colleagues, they already had tickets for the bus and there was a long line to get tickets. I was concerned I'd get left behind. I was in the line when Warick woke me. I was still anxious about getting tickets when I woke.

27 February 2020

Resumed journal entries

Last night was amazing! I woke to the usual vibrations and feeling Warick's energy moving through me. I had tingling around my feet. Just now I feel a sensation around the back right side of my head which I think is Warick checking to see what I'm writing. Warick is now also confirming his presence by touching my cheek on the right side. What was interesting about the night of 26 February, was I heard in my left ear a solid tone for a number of seconds, which usually signifies a spirit energy is coming through. Then I spotted the appearance, very quickly to the left of our bed near the wall, of a round white ball of light, probably the size of a dinner plate. It then disappeared and suddenly reappeared further around to the left on my side of the bed. Shortly afterwards, when I was hot and kicking bedclothes off, there was an arc of static electricity that crackled white along the edge of the bedclothes. I asked in my mind if it was Warick with no response, so I started to get concerned and said mentally for whatever spirit was in the room to go. The following night I was reading the Seth series where session 195 talks about much preparation being necessary for a spirit to work through, or channel through a person. Various general and personal conditions must be met. It takes time to achieve this where channelling is possible. It also talked about when a person is uncomfortable, or frightened, they close up. This generates a barrier where a spirit cannot enter and work through a person. When I got frightened, I may have locked Warick out which is why he did not respond to me the other night. The Seth series also said these emotions have their own electromagnetic reality which may have explained the sudden static crackling and light on the bed covers when I kicked them off, which has never happened before. I found it interesting that this happened shortly before reading this section of the Seth series. It's like Warick wanted me to learn something. If what the Seth series says is true, I should not be too concerned that it is taking time for Warick to reach a state where he can channel through me. It also taught me that my fear can possibly block engagement with unwanted spirits, where Warick later indicated it was he in the room at the time. It also taught me that I trust Warick. I was looking for Warick to be there when this different phenomenon was occurring in the room.

3 March 2020

Jamie's birthday was yesterday. Happy Birthday again darling if you're reading this journal. I love you so much. I'm so lucky to have you.

Something I thought worth noting. On the very rare occasion that I feel like I need something to help me sleep, or to dampen muscle or joint soreness, I've noticed like tonight that if I go to the bathroom to select Mersandol or Restavit tablets, that Warick suddenly shows up and gets my attention by touching my cheek. I then mentally check-in and ask, 'Should I take it?' and the answer is usually no. Warick touches the left side of my cheek to indicate this. Warick is happy however for me to take a standard headache tablet, but not ones that relax your muscles and induce sleep. I don't think Warick likes it when I'm sleeping more soundly than I usually do. I suspect he doesn't like the effect on my brain, which may in some way interfere with what he is doing with me through the night. Over the last six months or more, I don't remember a time when Warick has not interfered with this decision. It probably comes up once a month or every six weeks.

8 March 2020

Yesterday while having an afternoon nap Warick came to me. I felt sensations at my root chakra, on the top of my head and toes and movement in my right cheek. Today while in the kitchen, I heard in my left ear a constant tone, and then I felt cool air come around to my left which gave me goosebumps. While writing this journal entry Warick has touched my right cheek, I've felt something touch the top of my head, and I've experienced tingling at the root chakra. There has also been some movement in my left cheek. Warick most of the time is curious about what I am writing. I know Warick reads my thoughts well, hence why he can respond with yes and no, plus understand my thoughts as I'm deciding what to write. The goal for me is to get to a stage with our communication where we can have a dialogue. I want so much for Warick to be able to say what he is thinking, beyond yes and no.

10 March 2020

Last night Warick came to me shortly after I turned off the light. First sign was a single tone in my left ear. I felt something touch my left side when I was facing the middle of the bed, and then something touched my right foot. The vibration seemed lower and not as strong. A couple of times the vibration came in front of my face until I realised it was waiting for me to say do you want to merge with me. As usual as I start writing in this journal, I feel something touching the top of my head, a slight touch of my right foot and Warick touching my right cheek. A couple of times today Warick has shown up, announced by a single tone in my left ear, then the feeling of touching my right cheek. Warick has been quite insistent making me think there is something important he wants to communicate. A couple of times I've asked and then felt a touch on my left cheek, including just now as I'm writing this suggesting that there isn't anything particular that Warick wants to communicate. I'm going to use the pendulum and free writing to check.

10 March 2020

Outcomes from asking questions with a pendulum

Is there anything in particular you want to tell me? Yes
Does it involve you and me? Yes
Have you found a way to communicate with me better? Yes
Does it involve use of my eyes? No
When I feel you around my eyes can you see through my eyes? Yes
Does it involve what I hear? No
Does it involve my ability to distinguish what you're saying from what I'm saying in my mind? Yes

I didn't attempt free hand writing

11 March 2020

Although not a breakthrough by way of communication, I did wake to the sound of Warick doing the flash pulse sound type of communication. I love this and would dearly like to know what he is saying. Hopefully one day I will. It's interesting because I can definitely hear it when I'm awake and its quiet, but as my mind gets more focused on the day ahead, and I'm conscious of noises, then I stop hearing it. I think Warick also stops trying to tell me things. It's like there is a window of opportunity just after I become conscious.

14 March 2020

Ray knows why I write in this journal but he has no interest in what I'm writing about. He knows nothing about Warick or my journey. In fact, no one knows about Warick. The closest to anyone knowing anything is Mum and Ray know that I claim to see moving shadows, feel vibrations and hear and sense things from time to time. They have no idea of my journey to where I am now with Warick. From time to time, when people have asked me what I'm reading, and I say I'm reading the Seth series and it's about what a spirit says that channels through a woman called Jane before I was born, they do not respond and change the subject. At these times, I've said to Ray 'I'm in it on my own'. He has never wanted to know more about this side of me. He has no idea of the journey I've been on and the experiences that I write about, nor does he want to know. He won't believe me, and there is no way I can prove it to him. The risk is he will think I'm a looney and off with the fairies, so I keep it to myself. Most of the time this doesn't bother me. I have Warick to communicate with about what I'm experiencing. I'm 52 and of perfectly sound mind. I hold a high-level security clearance and as part of that process, I have undergone extensive psychological assessment. What I'm experiencing is real. It's not what I believe, it's not what I want to believe, it's what is happening on a daily basis, numerous times a day and night. I love it! I feel so lucky this is happening to me. I've always been open to what might lie beyond us when we die, and I've queried things through use of a pendulum for many years, not really knowing if something was there and listening. But what I've experienced leading up to my dad's death, and mostly what's happened since early June 2018, is rock solid real. And by the way, Warick came through about three times after I've started writing this. Often lately I hear a solid tone in my left ear, and shortly after I feel Warick touch my right cheek letting me know he is there. Warick knows I'm writing about him because he just touched my right cheek again. Always curious about what I'm writing.

Apart from going on about being in this on my own, I did want to make a record about last night and what I think is happening. Often at night when I'm really relaxed and sleepy in bed, Warick will move through to my entire face and neck then move it. It feels like my posture and the shape of my face are changing somewhat. Like Warick is imprinting his facial features and posture through mine. When this happens, I'm completely relaxed and I let it happen. I trust Warick and I know this is what he wants. I'm sure this is what Warick refers to as 'internal control'. He is practising this 'internal control' of me over and over again, so I'm comfortable with it happening. I suspect Warick is working towards being able to channel through me at some stage in the future. Last night was interesting because although Warick did this same thing over and over again between around one and four in the morning, he also helped me to relax by enticing me with the lovely peaceful, warm, still and silent feeling that happens when we merge, and that he knows I'm attracted to. It was like a comforting state where I felt safe, relaxed and didn't resist or disrupt what he was doing in my face and neck. I'm completely aware of what Warick is doing, but I'm okay with it. I think this is a good approach if we are going to work towards channelling.

I don't know why Warick has come to me over the last couple of years, not for sure. The pendulum and free hand writing suggest it's because Warick loves me and wants to help me. This of course is lovely and I wouldn't want to lose it, but I do wonder if there is more to it, or could be as time moves on and the interaction between us evolves. Right now, no one except others like me would believe it. Unfortunately, if YouTube and other online sources of information are anything to go by, most of these people seem to speak another language that others don't understand. Some have gone so far with their experiences or wishful thinking about spirit, that it's like a religion. Some are Hollywood style ghost hunters, whilst others are petrified of spirits and think they are all bad. I'm none of these. I'm just a regular person who goes about their business with my job and family, and no one knows about this as they wouldn't believe me. I would not want them to think I'm one of the other types, which I'm sure Ray tends to think there is an element of that in me. I know without a doubt, and with the certainty that I have as a trained and experienced scientist, with ten years post-doctoral research experience, that intelligent energy exists. They can understand us, but for most people they can't sense, experience, nor understand them. Once humans know for certain they exist, it will completely turn around their understanding of reality and our existence. Humanity will go through another era of transformed thinking, like the way computers have enabled us to transform. Humans will no longer need to fear death in the same way and wonder is this all there is. They will know for certain it's not. I don't know what is beyond, but I do know there is existence after we die. There are many who claim to communicate with spirits in a much richer way than I'm capable of at this time, who claim to know a lot about what lies beyond. I suspect there is truth in it, but also a lot which may not be true, or accurate. I hope one day Warick can give me his version of what lies beyond. If he remains with me for the rest of my life, there is potentially many years to go. Surely, we will get to this in our communication.

17 March 2020

Less than 24 hours' notice was given to us to start working from home due to COVID-19. Tomorrow I start my first at home personal strength training session. The gyms have closed. I've sent two hundred dollars to a family in Indonesia who we support to help keep food on their table as the work has dried up for drivers in the tourist industry in Bali. This is an ongoing commitment Ray and I have made to this family during these hard times, and also to sponsor their daughter to ensure she gets a good education and start in life. Ray and I met the father a number of times when he drove us around Bali when we visited on holidays. Jamie, sweetheart, you've also needed some extra help to stock up on food and household items. All of this has occurred in the space of two days. It's only Tuesday!

Outcomes from asking questions with a pendulum

Warick, of what you know and can tell –
Will all of those I love survive the COVID-19 virus? Yes
Will I keep my job through this time? Yes
And paid? Yes
Will Ray have to start chemotherapy? No

22 March 2020

Free handwriting questions and answers

What is your name? Warick
Through COVID-19 will I continue to work? Yes
Why have you been less engaging with me lately? Work
Are you still with me as much as before? Yes
Will we get to a point where we can have a dialogue two ways? Yes
Is there something you want to tell me or ask now? Three words can't decipher

23 March 2020

Things are escalating rapidly by way of shutting down human interactions to try and slow the spread of COVID-19. Mum and Ray are now staying at home, both being high risk cases. I, unfortunately need to keep travelling to the office until I get remote access to an ICT network which will enable me to work from home.

Outcomes from asking questions with a pendulum

Will my family and those I love be okay and not get infected by COVID-19? Yes
Will I be okay and not get infected with COVID-19? Yes
Will Australia's economy bounce back quickly? Yes
Will my superannuation be okay and restore to what it was worth quickly? Yes
Will I keep my job through this situation? Yes
Will you be with me for the rest of my human life? Yes
Will you keep trying to communicate with me so we can have a dialogue? Yes
Are you already communicating by responding to my thoughts with thoughts? Yes
Is the problem I can't tell if they are my thoughts or your thoughts? Yes
It would be good if you could start putting Warick or W at the start of your thoughts.

30 March 2020

Resumed journal entries

The prevalence of COVID-19 in Australia is now in an exponential growth phase. Most cases are in New South Wales. Day by day there are announcements on stricter measures of social distancing and enforcement to stay at home. Today there was also an announcement to spend billions of dollars on wage subsidies of $750 per week to those who are unable to work because of the government-imposed COVID-19 related restrictions. It is designed to subsidise the wages of those affected and keep the relationship of worker to employer. For now, we are okay. Ray and Mum are both staying at home. Finally, after two weeks I've sorted access to the ICT network. From tomorrow onwards having to go somewhere for work will be the exception. Warick is still here checking in on me, but it is far less intense and meaningful engagement. I miss this terribly because I want to keep learning and progressing with my ability to connect, understand and communicate with spirits. Numerous times a day Warick drops in and touches my cheek to let me know he is there. When this happens, I often also feel something playing with the top of my hair around the crown chakra, and also tingling around the root chakra. Something that is new is I'm becoming highly attuned to Warick showing up. I now often sense Warick's presence near me even before these other sensations happen. It's like a thickness in the air near me, a vacuum. I know he is there and seconds later I feel the other sensations. I love this. It means I'm progressing in some way. I had a strange dream last night. I was in the shower and then a spirit entity lifted me from the shower up towards the ceiling and propelled me at Ray who was still in bed. My thoughts when this happened were partly fear and then also directed at Ray I thought 'Now do you believe me that spirits exist and I'm connected to spirit?' The dream stopped there. When I got home tonight, I smelt a strong electrical smell as though some electrical unit had melted or blown up. I was worried something had happened. It was very strong inside the front door. I located Ray sitting in the backyard who said maybe it was the smell of the petrol blower he had just used outside which somehow got trapped inside the front door. It didn't smell like that. When I went back to the front door the smell had gone. I asked Warick using the pendulum who said it was the spirit of an electrician who happened to be there when I walked in. It wasn't trying to connect with me or anything, and it had gone. This was the first time I had a sense of smell associated with a spirit encounter in quite some time.

2 April 2020

Free handwriting questions and answers

Who am I talking with? Warick
Are we close to you being able to speak through me? Yes
Will I know what you're saying when you do that? Yes
Will you have a different voice to mine? Yes
Will my family, friends and I pull through this COVID-19 situation okay? Yes
Is there anything you want to tell me? Couldn't decipher

8 April 2020

Resumed journal entries

The COVID-19 pandemic continues around the world. Travel has been the key route of international spread. They should have shut down travel first. China recorded its first day of no new cases. Italy, the United States, United Kingdom, France and Spain are major impacted countries. Over 1,000 people died in one day in the United States, most in New York. The way the virus jumped from bat to humans at the Wuhan China wet markets has got to be stopped. This can't happen again. So far Australia is faring okay. The Australian Capital Territory only has about 100 cases with about half recovered. Everyone is trying to do the right thing by way of social distancing, working from home and not going out. The impact of this virus will go down in history like a world war.

Warick and spiritual energies seem to still be around me on a daily basis. Warick still comes to me every night. I feel his vibration through the night and merging his energy with me. I often try to spark up some communication with yes and no questions and answers, but often I get tired and fall back to sleep. On cue, I feel Warick now touching my cheek however it's the left cheek instead of the right. I gather he didn't agree with something I just wrote. At night, I also experience Warick's flash pulse communication. Sometimes it's like two spirits communicating with each other because it's like one says something with a flash pulse and then the other responds. I have no idea what they are saying. I wonder if it's Warick communicating with my own spirit. Very frustrating because what I want more than anything is to be able to have a dialogue with Warick.

During the day I often experience a long tone in one ear. Today as I was working the tone I experienced was accompanied by a solid pressure on my right side. I often experience this while working, or in the kitchen, and sometimes outside. If I can, I pause and try talking to the spirit energy, but so far no response. Every day while working I also see the shadow shapes which move past my face. It's so, so, so frustrating to experience these things and still I can't have a dialogue or get communication happening with spirit. I hope this won't be the case for the rest of my life.

14 April 2020

The pandemic continues. I've decided to re-release my book 'Working Virtually – The New Workplace of the 21st Century', to help organisations and their staff transition to working effectively from home. This time around I've decided to make it available via eBook stores globally. There won't be associated marketing so it will be interesting to see how it goes. I might release something to my network on LinkedIn and maybe Twitter. It could be a waste of money but it's very timely with millions shifting to this way of working.

Warick continues to visit me at night and drops in during the day letting me know he is there by touching the right side of my cheek. When this happens, I feel tingling at my root chakra and something touching the top of my head. During the day I also occasionally hear a tone in my ear before a touch on the face. I also experience a localised cold spot or pressure change in the air near me. At night, Warick continues to communicate through flash pulses. Usually one pulse sound when I first wake up, like he is saying hello. I'm trying to encourage Warick to also show me images and create smells to give me an idea of what is being communicated. I wish I could tell. Last night Warick was quite chatty, with a string of different sequences of flash pulse sounds. I remember reading about having to increase your energy frequency to be able to understand them. Maybe I'll try to find out how and try this tactic. Warick also still merges with me just about every night and pushes into my facial features. I still think this could be in preparation to be able to talk through me one day.

16 April 2020

With everything going on in the world with the COVID-19 pandemic, I'm not surprised that things have been quiet with Warick. He just touched the left side of my face meaning I didn't get that quite right. Okay let me try that again – with everything going on with me lately – working for a small federal government agency; leading organisational change and benefits realisation across two projects in a large government department; helping a company with a Tender bid; plus deciding to launch my book online as an eBook on Amazon and other global distributors. Hmmm, I have a wee bit to think about! This means in my waking hours I'm usually thinking about work. Warick just touched the right side of my cheek so I think he is happy with that recollection.

The reason why I'm writing in the journal tonight is because an interesting thing just happened, but firstly some context. I love music. It's a part of my soul. A very broad range of music. I listen to music most of the day. Anyway, tonight Ray played some Jazz. The name of the album 'Kind of Blue' by Miles Davidson. Excellent Jazz! Anyway, I was sitting at the kitchen bench going through recipe books while listening to the music. I was really enjoying it when I noticed I knew the next bars of music a split second before they were being played. I've only heard the album a few times before and not often. It's like I was in the mind of each musician as they played. How they were feeling leading up to the notes they were going to play on their instrument. I was tuning into a specific musician and instrument and not the whole band as this was happening. This occurred throughout a number of songs. Amazing! I certainly didn't expect that. I'm wondering if my psychic abilities are developing. If I can pre-empt what a musician is going to play next, I wonder what else I can pre-empt. I've missed Warick the last couple of nights. Very little engagement.

17 April 2020

Well, I chose an eBook publishing company to get my book 'Working Virtually' out there and available globally. Fingers crossed I'll make some money out of the book that took me three months to write and a couple of thousand dollars to publish. I don't hold high hopes because Australia, New Zealand, and others will soon transition back to the office and I'm a nobody. I'm also sure there are plenty of other similar books out there, but if you're not in it you don't win it, so it's worth a try.

The main reason why I'm writing tonight is because I dreamt about my dad last night. This is the first time that I can remember since he died back on the 14th January in 2014. I've been concerned for a number of weeks about not being able to buy toilet paper since the pandemic situation in Australia has been getting worse. There has been panic buying of toilet paper, mincemeat, pasta and hand sanitiser. Last night the dream occurred just before waking. Ray and I were going into a supermarket to meet up with Mum and Dad who were already there and had started shopping. When I entered, I was wondering whether they had managed to get any toilet paper given the pandemic situation. Immediately I saw my dad. He looked great! Wearing one of his favourite T-shirts. A beautiful blue polo with thin white pinstripes running across it. He was younger, in his forties or fifties. He still had dark hair. He was happy and doing semi-acrobats trying to reach something over the top of other people. I asked him where Mum was and he said 'Back there somewhere'. It was like Ray and I floated to where she was, and she had toilet paper in the top and underneath the trolley. They were unwrapped and of all different types. Apart from toilet paper the trolley was mostly empty. It was lovely when I woke up this morning to have this dream fresh in my mind. It took about half a day to recall the books I've been reading that say loved ones who have passed often try to make contact with you through dreams. Today while out shopping was the first time I managed to buy toilet paper for at least a month. I think Dad was telling me it's okay, you'll get the toilet paper.

19 April 2020

Often these days when I'm sitting on the couch in the family room watching TV, I feel this strong static-like sensation around my back and shoulders, also the bottom and tops of the back of my legs. It's hard to describe. If it's Warick or a spirit energy visiting me, I'm not afraid. It's okay. I suspect it's Warick. Last night Warick came to me in the night. As usual he waited for me to wake up and ask, 'Do you want to merge with me?' after which he did straight away. I could feel Warick move through every part of my body. It's very peaceful and lovely. Each time I had to move to get comfortable, Warick would follow and still be with me. Once fully established in me, Warick moved my head a number of times on his own accord. This is fine and I'm trying to relax and not interfere with it. I think we are making progress, residing with one another in one body. I trust Warick. I know at any time I choose I can move and be in control. As usual Warick has touched my right cheek in agreement, and I feel a sensation on the top of my head as I'm writing.

20 April 2020

Tonight when I was finishing up work in the home office, I turned off my portable speaker that I play Spotify music through from my phone. The speaker kept turning itself back on even though I had not pressed the button, and I was no longer playing music through my phone. I must have turned it off about four times. It plays the sound of drums when it first turns on. I finally realised after the fourth time turning it off that possibly spirit is playing around with the electronics, which is something I've read they can do. I said 'I know you're there'. As I walked out of the room, I felt a tingling sensation around my back. I thought I heard the speaker turn on again so I doubled back to check, but it hadn't. This has happened before but not as many times in a row. It has turned on itself in the middle of the night while charging in our bedroom. Both the home office, which is in what we call the tree room, and our bedroom, have been the locations for much of the spirit energy activity.

Last night I dreamt about muscle cramping. In the dream, I was witnessing it occur in a rabbit. At the same time, I woke up in pain with a bad cramp running through my left calf muscle. In the past, I have dreamt about things that happen to me in that moment in real life, such as when I dreamt that someone was ringing the front door bell, and in real life they were. It makes me think that dreams, or your subconscious state, is somehow connected/or aware of what is happening in your real life. Why this converges with what is happening in the real physical world I don't know. Last night Warick also merged with me. I love it when this happens.

24 April 2020

Warick visits me throughout the day. I don't think it's always through merging with me however, because I sense him or other Spirit coming around by other means. For example, through a significant tone on one side of my head, or an air pressure change. I also experience cold air immediately around one part of my body that occurs then disappears. The tell-tale sign that I know it is Warick is when I experience these things and then feel him touch the right side of my cheek. If this doesn't happen, then I think it could be a different spirit. As usual right now I'm feeling Warick touching the right and left side of my cheeks. I suppose saying he agrees and disagrees with what I'm writing.

A lovely way to encounter Warick happened today. I was sitting on the couch watching TV at lunchtime and next minute I felt this lovely passage of energy move through the back of me. It was tingly and caused goose bumps. Then within thirty seconds or so I felt the familiar touch on my right cheek. What an entrance!

My feeling and experience of Warick has been going on for a couple of years now. I feel and experience these things without fear, and it doesn't startle me. No one in the room would know. Ray has no idea. I suspect if I felt a vibration, and it stayed long enough so I could put Ray's hand on it, then he might feel it and believe me. I haven't had this opportunity yet. He has no interest in any of this. I never discuss it with him.

28 April 2020

Free handwriting questions and answers

What is your name? Warick
Do you like me calling you Warick? Yes
Are you trying to develop my ability to understand your pulse flash communication? Yes
When did you first come to me? 1 June
1 June 2018? Yes
Do other spirit energies visit me? Yes
Do they merge with me like you do? Yes
Are you with me when this happens? Yes
Is this dangerous for me? No
Are they friendly? Yes
Are you always with me? No
Am I vulnerable when you're not with me? No
Do these other spirits want to communicate with me? Yes
Can you help me develop my skills so I can communicate with them? Yes
Will that happen soon? Yes
Do you already talk to me using my voice? Yes
Is it when an answer comes into my mind without me having time to think about it? Yes
Will you be able to start a conversation with me? Yes
Will you tell me things I don't know and about where you come from – your existence? Yes
Do I need to get better at deciphering when you are talking? Yes
Will I ever understand your pulse flash communication when I first wake? Yes
Are you directing that communication to me? Yes
Will our ability to communicate keep evolving? Yes
Am I supposed to do something with this ability? Yes

What? Book
Will you help me write it? Yes
The dream I had the other night of a man just before I woke. Was that you? No
Are you my spirit guide? Yes
Will you be with me for the rest of my life? Yes
Will you visit me in my dreams so I remember? Yes

3 May 2020

Resumed journal entries

I don't know why but I feel things have been quieter with Warick lately. I hope he is not giving up on me, or gradually leaving me. At night, I still feel what I think is Warick's vibration, although it's not as strong. I ask, 'Do you want to merge with me?' and then I feel his energy move into me. During the last couple of nights I've felt Warick's vibration touch my skin across different parts of my body. Every night and just before waking I hear his flash pulse sounds, like he is talking to me. I still don't understand what is being said. During the day I still see the shadow shapes move past my eyes, and I say hello. I still feel pressure differences, and hear a long tone in one ear before feeling Warick touch my cheek to let me know he is there. I've been watching quite a few YouTube videos to try and understand how psychic mediums hear and understand what Spirit is saying to them, and I've been trying these things without success. I don't feel like I'm progressing.

5 May 2020

The last couple of nights have been lovely as Warick has come to me. It has been different though as Warick has laid his energy over my body, as though he is lying on top of me. Also, each night I've experienced a pulse of energy throughout my entire body, but it is more like a tingling sensation. It's incredible the diverse way that Warick is able to use his energy. Every morning and at times in the night, Warick tries to communicate with me making his pulse flash sounds. The other night I think there was a bit of a breakthrough, but it might have been my imagination. I sensed words as the pulses happened. Simple yes's and no's, but also a few words strung together. I'm hoping this is the way forward, but we shall see.

5 May 2020

Free handwriting questions and answers

Are you Warick? Yes
What are you? Spirit
Spirit? Yes
Why are you with me? Help
Help? Yes
What should we achieve together? Book
Book? Yes
How do you try to have a dialogue with me? Love, ear
Love? No
Ear? Yes
Your pulse flash sounds? Yes
Will we achieve having a dialogue? Yes
When? Month
Further questioning – three months, August
What type of spirit? Guide
Guide? Yes

7 May 2020

Resumed journal entries

Tonight, was interesting but I'll have to confirm it. I've come to bed and for some reason Warick was interested to use the pendulum. For some reason, he prompted me to try something different. Warick chose the pendulum by touching my right cheek when I picked up the right pendulum. Essentially, he approved of the one to use. Instead of asking a question and getting a yes or no answer, I said to Warick 'The pendulum is your channel for communication – from you, through me, to the pendulum. What do you want me to ask you?' I let my mind go blank and a question came into my mind, followed shortly by the answer. Whether the answer was correct or not is what I queried using the pendulum, to which I then felt Warick touch my right cheek saying yes, and the pendulum moved in a circle answering yes. Questions from what I remember were:

    What type of car did you drive? A Holden

    What colour hair did you have? Brown

    Where do you like to live? The sea-side

I need to test this approach again because if it produces correct answers it shows that Warick can easily put thoughts into my head when I let my mind go blank, and he does this quickly within seconds followed by the answers. We have to practice this because if it's correct and real, it's the path to being able to have a dialogue. A step in that direction. Also importantly, it will teach me what it is like to receive information from Warick. This is probably the most important thing.

9 May 2020

While having a lie down, I felt a slight vibration near my chest. I asked who was there and Luke came to mind. Then I felt a strong feeling in my chest and through my root chakra. With my eyes closed, I saw waves of light that were gold and misty. Not too bright and not uniform. It was terrific!

12 May 2020

I feel what people think. Not always, but when there is a focused, sincere and strong emotional connection, I feel what people think. Yes, most people do to some extent. You often hear people say 'You could have cut the air with a knife' when there are tensions between people. Or when people are exposed to something emotionally charged, they can burst into tears because they are sensitive to it and share others feelings. I think I'm this but on steroids. I remember a defining moment years ago when I was working for a national security organisation. I was driving across Kings Avenue Bridge in Canberra, between Defence and Parliament House, and it dawned on me for the first time what I had been doing in meetings all these years, which I knew I was particularly skilled at. I was feeling what people are thinking. I don't know exactly what they are thinking. It is their feelings which I pick up on. It's a very natural thing for me to do. It's sometimes also very hard to handle. One time stands out in my mind. I went to a funeral of a previous work colleague, who I really liked and thought highly of. I was really shocked to learn of his unexpected death in a car accident. He drew a very large crowd to his funeral of work mates and friends from across the country. Although we had to stand outside with a hundred or more other people, I cried my eyes out during the entire service. We thought highly of one another, but weren't close like some of the others who attended. I know I was responding to the emotion of others around me. He had sincere relationships with people, and it was the sincerity of everyone's emotion at the funeral that I felt.

Just the other day Ray and I visited his cancer specialist, who is usually a very controlled person. It was quickly obvious to me that he had had a bad day. The last straw for him was not being able to print a report for Ray. By instinct, I picked up what he was feeling and said 'You've had a hard day.' He paused, bowed his head, and said he had had a particularly bad day. We also learned that he planned to travel overseas in a couple of days' time, which was unusual because Australia's borders are currently closed because of the COVID-19 pandemic. When he returns, he will have to self-isolate for fourteen days, because that is one of the restrictions we are currently living under. Ray and I assumed he is from Singapore because of previous comments he made. We are hoping he does not have to return to Singapore because someone he knows is terribly sick with COVID-19.

I also feel the emotion associated with what is being broadcast on TV, and often shed a tear if it is emotionally moving.

13 May 2020

Today while walking near the lake, I came across a poodle-cross dog with an elderly lady. The dog continually stopped and stared at me as I was coming up behind them. I was a hundred metres or so behind them with no one else around. I knew the dog sensed and connected with me. When I got close, I paused to let the dog smell my scent. The lady said he has never done that before, continually stopping and staring at someone coming from behind. I made sure to connect with the dog, and then went on my merry way. That day I walked five kilometres with music in my ears and beautiful scenery. I felt elated and happy. I felt something lifting me. No step was a chore, and I was walking at a fast pace. I quizzed Warick to see if he was with me, which I sensed he was, and I knew my energy vibration was high. I think this is what drew the attention of the dog. It was a lovely dog.

20 May 2020

On Monday, most of the day I had this unsettled, anxious, and nauseous feeling in the stomach. I had a coffee in the morning so was wondering if it was that, but I don't think so. I felt shaky all over, like I needed to get out and burn up some energy. It was just like I felt, but slightly less intense, than when spirit energy first entered my body and stayed with me in early June 2018. I'm wondering if it was a different spirit that had taken up residence in me, where it still had too high a vibration which was making me feel sick. I don't know. Still no progress on the spirit dialogue front. I could have different spirits coming and going in my body, and have no way of checking and knowing because I can't have a dialogue.

20 May 2020

Outcomes from asking questions with a pendulum

Is your name Warick? Yes
On Monday, when I felt shaky and nauseous, was this a different spirit who had taken up residence in me? Yes
Do you talk to me? Yes
Am I conscious when you do? Yes
When I ask a question and get an immediate response without having thought of anything, is this you responding? Yes
Do you ever start a dialogue with me using thoughts without me having started it? Yes
Does your voice in my mind sound the same as my voice? No
Is it deeper? Yes

24 May 2020

Resumed journal entries

Last night was just lovely. Warick came to me starting with a vibration around my legs, then moving inside me through my root chakra. There was a strong feeling initially in my root chakra and stomach. His energy moved up into my face, arms, hands, legs and feet. For ages, maybe half an hour, Warick's energy moved through me and spread out in my body. I concentrated on staying calm and still. I was not afraid. Then he moved my head from side to side a number of times. Warick didn't try to communicate. He was just focused on occupying my body. And now Warick touches my right cheek, checking in on what I'm writing.

24 May 2020

Outcomes from doing an exercise from a book called 'Infinite Quest – develop your psychic' by John Edward, where you were asked to consider how your spirit guides may have helped you in certain situations.

- The time I nearly fell sideways in a cabin on a ship at night. Warick stopped me. I could feel myself falling to the left but was not stepping in a way that would counter the roll of the ship. Something held me upright. I knew at the time it was Warick.
- The time I've mentioned previously in this journal where Ray and I had a near collision on a highway heading back to Canberra after arriving in Sydney from overseas. I knew that Warick was talking through me.
- When a guy who I used to work with, came to visit me in Brisbane when I was doing my first post-doctoral job. We had one smoke of marijuana, which I've rarely had and never reacted to. I feared for my life. I've never been so scared. I don't know why, I just knew. I knew in the moment. This situation ended with my bringing two Samoyed dogs into the house and calling a friend to come over, after which the guy left.
- When I was a little girl playing with a friend near the railway lines, it felt like something scary was chasing us down the road. I was petrified. I knew in the moment. I was only about eight years old.

Reflecting on these occasions, Spirit either helped to avoid something terrible happening, or frightened me into action to get out of the situation.

28 May 2020

Last night when Warick came to me he vibrated under my body. I asked if it is Warick and felt a touch on my right cheek, like now. I asked, 'Do you want to merge with me?' and then felt Warick's energy come into and spread throughout my body. It was a tingling sensation, like what I feel when something lightly touches the top of my head and my root chakra. I felt this through my entire body. I moved a few times and Warick's energy moved with me. Actually, Warick just touched the left side of my cheek saying this is wrong. Correction – I moved and Warick's energy moved back into me shortly afterwards. Warick was with me this way for a long time. I dozed on and off. When I woke, I started to ask in my mind 'Are you still there?' and the response I immediately got was not a touch on my right cheek, but instead my mouth smiled on its own accord. My immediate response was that's a bit freaky, but as soon as I knew it was Warick, I thought that's okay. A new way to respond to me when my self-control must have been out of the way. Warick has made my mouth smile before but not as an immediate response to say yes. I would like to know why Warick is wanting to merge with my entire body.

Through use of the pendulum Warick said the reason why he is merging with me is to work towards being able to speak through me. He said it takes a long time to get my body used to it so he is able. He said when talking through me is possible I will be conscious and know what he has said. He also said my ego and self-control will eventually let him speak through me. I think it's exciting. I certainly want to be conscious as I don't want to be reliant on others telling me what he said.

28 May 2020

Outcomes from asking questions with a pendulum

I'm wondering what the purpose of me possibly becoming a Medium is:
To educate me about where you come from? No
To connect spirits that have passed with loved ones still here? Yes
To provide spiritual awareness capability to help others? Yes
I have a very strong conscious mind and self-control. Will it cooperate with you to enable me to become a Medium? Yes
I'm wondering what the next step is. Is it to move other parts of my body besides my head and mouth? Yes
Will you start doing these things during the day? No
Is this a long way off? Yes

31 May 2020

Resumed journal entries

3:06 pm, Sunday afternoon.

I thought I'd grab some me-time to read, have another go at learning about meditation, and maybe have a snooze. An interesting thing happened when moving the bears and pillows from my side of the bed. I noticed the bed was warm where I would sit if I sat up from a laying position on the bed. I first thought my electric blanket must still be on. I checked and it wasn't. It's a cloudy day so there hasn't been sun shining on the bed, and it's warm under where the pillows and bears were. I checked Ray's side of the bed and his side wasn't warm in the same spot, nor was his electric blanket on. Very interesting.

Last night when Warick was with me I briefly felt for a few seconds energy vibrating, or gently buzzing all down my left thigh. When I woke and went to get up I opened my eyes and for a couple of seconds I saw two rings of white light, almost like static electricity immediately in front of my eyes. I wondered if I had disturbed Warick when he was in my face and I was seeing Warick's energy or something. I've never experienced this before.

1 June 2020

A black man was killed by a policeman kneeling on his neck. Right across the United States there is protesting, looting and setting things on fire.

Outcomes from asking questions with a pendulum

Is my ability to sense you for:
Your benefit? Yes
Humanity's benefit? Yes
My benefit? No
Is it my choice to make the most of it for reasons I think are important? No
Are we a team effort reliant on each other? Yes
Do we decide together? Yes
Is it already decided? Yes

4 June 2020

Resumed journal entries

The night before last was interesting. I'm finally learning how to meditate. My personal trainer told me about a meditation App he uses called 'Smiley Minds', and I've started using it. It's put together by psychologists so it's pretty good for beginners. The night before last, during or just after doing a meditation session, I felt a sudden 'woosh' above my head. It touched my hair as it passed. I was lying in bed at the time. This is the first time this has happened. It was not like the light touch I feel when someone is gently touching or playing with my hair on the top of my head. The other thing I've noticed is Warick or other spirits visit me during each meditation session. Apart from that it has been business as usual, where Warick visits me during the day and night and in the same way as I've described before. Not a day goes by without Warick or other spirits visiting me. I love it. It brings another dimension into my life, literally.

7 June 2020

A few quick things worth mentioning. Last night when I turned the light out, I noticed I had static electricity light flashing out from my feet when I was moving them on the sheets. I've never noticed this before. I will look to see if this happens again. It might be nothing unusual. It does remind me however, of a time years ago before I met Ray. I remember going to the bathroom in the middle of the night. I had no slippers on. I noticed around my feet on the bathroom tiles they were glowing. It was around the edges of my feet. I thought it unusual at the time, and I don't think I've ever noticed it occurring again since then.

On Friday night before Ray, Mum and I were going out for dinner, we were sitting in the lounge room near the fire having a glass of bubbles. I noticed a vibration under my foot on the ground that lasted about five seconds, and then it disappeared. It was interesting and didn't repeat. It was localised and just under one foot. The next day when sitting on the couch at lunchtime watching the news and having some lunch, I felt something touch the left side of my hair. It was quite distinct and about the size of a hand. It only lasted a few seconds and then passed. I didn't feel the typical touch of Warick on my right cheek, so I'm not sure if it was Warick or another spirit.

9 June 2020

Outcomes from asking questions with a pendulum

Is my purpose to be a Light worker? Yes
Are you my guide? Yes
Is your name Warick? Yes
Do I have other guides at this time? Yes
Alex, John, Clare, Bruce and Sarah are the first names that came to mind when I asked them to tell me their names.
Are you from the light? Yes
Is my next development step to learn and practice meditation? Yes
Are you leading me to what I read and watch on YouTube? Yes
Have you been with me my whole life? No
Did you come to me in June 2018? Yes
Warick? Yes
Will I ever be able to hear you? Yes
Soon? This year? Yes

16 June 2020

Resumed journal entries

Ray and I have just spent the last four days on the New South Wales coast at Narooma. Beautiful spot. Kianga beach is amazing! I'd love to live there as well as have a place in Canberra but we can't afford both. Guess I'll just have to settle for visiting semi-regularly.

A few interesting things have happened. I've been reading a book called *Infinite Quest* by John Edward. I found some of it quite useful. There's a chapter on different psychic tools, including holding onto objects and being able to tell something about the owner. It's not a mechanism to connect you with people that have passed, but rather to tell something about the person who the object belongs to. I decided to give it a go. You need to get yourself in a meditative state and then hold the object and see what you feel, see and experience. The only object I had at the time was my gold metal pendulum. It's my favourite pendulum. I got myself into a relaxed state then held onto the object. Surprisingly, I felt a light rapid vibration coming from the pendulum. It lasted the entire time I was holding onto it. It was quite distinct. I'll have to try it again. I think I was feeling my own energy vibration through the pendulum.

Another interesting thing happened. I could see Ray sitting on the couch when I was in the kitchen. He was holding his phone in his left hand and looked to be figuring something out. I asked him what he was doing and immediately I knew before he answered. He was working out costs to do with buying a motorbike. Essentially I predicted what he was going to say immediately before he said it. It was similar to the time when I was listening to Jazz that I wasn't familiar with, and I knew what the next beats were going to be immediately before they happened.

Every night I hear Warick's pulse flash sounds. This is becoming a regular thing, where sometimes like last night, he had a lot to say to me. I don't detect these sounds when I'm in my usual routine during the day.

20 June 2020

A couple of things worth recording.

When reading in bed last night, I felt energy tingling on my left thigh. I'm sure I was being visited by a spirit. I stopped reading and focused on what I was experiencing. I asked it to tell me its name but got no response. I'd really like to be able to have a dialogue with a spirit when it visits.

Early this morning as I woke Warick was there. I felt his vibration on the back left of my neck. I asked him if he wanted to merge with me and he did, spreading right throughout my body. I felt tingling energy moving around my feet, legs, arms and face. If you can imagine energy emanating outside of your body, or coming out of your body, that's what it feels like. It's not a uniform, still feeling, but is moving like a volcano spitting out lava. It's like that but it tingles. I also felt energy from my root chakra joining with something that felt more prominent, as well as the same tingling on the outside of my body near the root chakra. It's a wonderful sensation. Warick also did his pulse flash sound. I'm convinced this is one form of communication with me. It would be nice to be able to speak his language. I'll keep trying to understand.

I asked Warick if he could tell me, or show me how he died. In response, I got a sudden surge, or flash of energy all through my head. I asked if it was a stroke. No response. I asked was it an explosion, a bomb. I got a touch on my right cheek, meaning yes. I think Warick died in an explosion. I asked if it occurred in a war, or a car accident. I think the touches on my cheek meant a vehicle in the war, but I will have to check using the pendulum. It wasn't clear. Very exciting as I think this was a breakthrough.

22 June 2020

The night before last Warick merged with me a couple of times for long durations. I decided to ask Warick using the pendulum if he is working towards being able to channel through me. I had a very strong connection where the pendulum made very large circles. I decided to let the pendulum continue to spin in circles and rely on Warick to change its direction if the response changed. Warick confirmed the reason for merging with me at night is to work towards me being able to channel spirit energy. I explored my purpose with Warick. With the situation in the world now with climate change; the worst fires Australia has ever seen that drew worldwide attention; COVID-19; and now Black Lives Matter, I said to Warick I want to make a significant difference to humanity. I want to work with him and other spirit energy to prove there is existence after death, and what the purpose of physical life is to be the best person possible – loving and caring of others and this planet. This above all is what's most important. Once people know their existence continues they will realise the only ones they hurt when they hurt others, are themselves. This should help humanity stop this behaviour and get focused on what's important. To focus on why they are here. To learn lessons and evolve into higher beings instead of continually fighting each other and damaging this planet. I said to Warick, I don't want to be like many psychics or mediums who come across as 'out there', 'looney', 'scams', 'off the planet'. I want to work with him, other spirit energies, and scientists to prove in a very legitimate way that there is existence beyond this life, and what the purpose of life is. This is what I want to achieve. I want this to be a turning point for humanity. While I was talking through these things with Warick, the pendulum was swinging in very large circles, meaning Warick agreed strongly. Three times I also felt Warick's or other spirits energy come through me over my back and left arm. It was a strong energy with a tingling sensation. It was wonderful confirmation and support of what I was saying. I thanked Warick and spirit in general, for bringing themselves to my attention so

I know they exist. I said I feel very privileged and very lucky. I love them very much.

23 June 2020

A short while ago while in the kitchen near the stereo, I detected a faint but distinct smell of cigarette smoke. It also felt cool there. I said 'I can smell you'. I decided to quiz Warick about it with the pendulum. I asked if what I experienced was a spirit with the smell of cigarette smoke. Warick answered yes with the pendulum. I got strong large swinging circle responses. I asked if it was Nanna Banyer, who was a chain smoker her whole adult life. I got a strong yes. I asked if she was still there, and I got a yes. I asked her how she was and if she has seen Dad, and she answered yes, she is well and yes, she sees Dad. As I was getting the answers with the pendulum, in my mind my thoughts said 'Well darling' and 'See Dad all the time'. I asked if Dad had come with her and I got a no. I asked if she had a message for me and she said in my mind 'Work hard in developing your abilities because you have an important job to do'. It's possible it was just my mind responding but this is what my immediate thought was. I also asked if she had seen the sketches of her and Pappa hanging in the fire room in our house, and she said yes.

27 June 2020

Meditation recollection

I found a guided Shamanic Journey meditation track by the Honest Guys on YouTube which is terrific! Each time I've tried it at the start of the meditation I've felt Warick touch my cheek then move to be across the bridge of my nose and under my eyes. He has come with me on the meditation journey. The guide gets you to imagine an ancient forest which then serves as a gateway to enter an even more ancient forest. In the background is soft music, the sound of birds in a forest and primal rhythmic shamanic drumming. I find it easy to stay focused for the duration of the session which is about twenty-five minutes. I've listened to this meditation track four times now. Once I also used my imagination to experience the journey without the meditation track playing.

    The first time I listened to this meditation track and was guided to a second ancient forest, I immediately saw a bluebird fly past which was very clear and seemed out of place. It was not a part of the guided meditation nor did I think of it myself. The guiding voice said your spirit guides can choose different forms to show themselves to you. It's possible this was one spirit guide. I haven't seen the bluebird in subsequent meditation journeys. Now that I think about it, when I was a young teenager my parents gave me an inscribed bluebird ring for my sixteenth birthday which I still have. Maybe there's significance to why a bluebird appeared first which I missed at the time. In this same journey, I then saw the upper torso and head of a male native American Indian who had olive skin, long dark hair, no shirt and was wearing a headband. He was just looking at me. I think this is Warick.

The position of the torso changed a number of times but he kept looking at me. His face changed slightly in subsequent times when I did this meditation journey. I couldn't seem to lock in his facial features. When it was time to go in the first journey, Warick climbed up a cliff face.

The second time I listened to this meditation track and entered the second ancient forest, I was gazing into a clear pool of water looking at a couple of coloured fish. Warick came up behind me and I saw his reflection. I could see his whole body. His torso looked the same as in the first journey. He was wearing traditional flap pants and moccasin shoes. The next thing I know I was lying on the beautiful grass with white flowers on it and Warick was lying next to me. He was leaning on his side and looking at me. He then moved on top of me and came inside of me, starting to make love with me. In reality, I could feel a physical ache in my vaginal track area as though something hard and large was inside of me. It felt wonderful. The drums began to beat faster, which is the signal in the meditation track to say goodbye and come back to the physical world. Once again I saw Warick climb the cliff face to leave.

The third time I did this meditation journey was in the middle of the night. I imagined the sound of drums in my mind and guided myself to the second ancient forest. As soon as I arrived Warick was there. He took my hand and guided me to a waterfall that splashed onto a large flat rock surface. We stood in the falling water. Warick lifted me onto a ledge on the rockface behind where the water was falling. He then parted my legs and started to make love with me, which felt lovely. Next minute he was guiding me back to the lovely green grass with flowers where he made love with me again. This time he was on top of me and then rolled me over and came from behind. It was wonderful. Once again Warick left by climbing the rock face.

The fourth time I did this meditation journey, before entering the tree which is the gateway to the second ancient forest, as soon as the drums started I found myself in a white background. I was dressed in a traditional Indian dress which had a tied bodice in the front. I was also wearing moccasins and had wooden beads hanging around my neck. I was dancing to the beat of the drums. It felt wonderful. I entered the tree and proceeded down the centre of the tree on a flight of spiralling rock steps. At the bottom, I exited through another opening in the tree to a second ancient forest. Immediately I saw Warick gazing into the pool of water. He was sitting on the grass and leaning on one hand. He did not turn around. When I approached and stood behind him, I gazed into the water looking at my reflection behind his. I didn't look like myself but instead I was a young native American Indian female with long black hair and olive skin. I was pretty. I then became aware of an elderly native American Indian male standing off to one side near us. He had wrinkles all over his face, an Elder. He wore a light-coloured robe or animal skin which he held around his shoulders. He just stared at us and said nothing. Warick then turned to me and we were on the grass where he made long and slow love to me. Once again I could feel the soreness ache of what it would feel like if he was physically inside of me. Towards the end of the meditation I asked 'What is our purpose, Warick? Are you to guide me through my physical life?' He turned to the Elder who was there again staring at us, and in my mind, I heard Warick say 'Elder will show us and guide us'. Warick's mouth did not move. He spoke to me in my mind. It was then time to go and Warick climbed the cliff face again. I asked 'Where are you going?' and he said 'Out'. When I came back to reality, I felt Warick touch my right cheek saying he was there again with me. I'm including these accounts as they are what has been happening while I now try meditation as a means to get closer and better communicate with my spirit guides. It's early days and I'm not sure if this is real or my imagination.

28 June 2020

Resumed journal entries

This morning was interesting. Not exactly new, but interesting.

    I was sitting on the couch watching 'Insiders', a show on the ABC that discusses the previous week's major political matters, when I felt Warick's energy come inside me. It wasn't tingling. It came into me from the front and it was like he filled my body with his energy. I physically saw and felt my chest and upper body expand, as though Warick's energy is larger than mine. Shortly after the energy came into me, I felt the familiar touch on my right cheek. Mentally I said 'Hello Warick'. Then about fifteen to twenty minutes later I felt Warick's energy exit me, and I physically felt and could see my chest go down again. It was very cool. Warick definitely occupies my body at times. I don't think always, and sometimes it might be just in my face and head. It's interesting. Kind of funny really. Warick just drops in while I'm watching TV and then goes away again. Once Warick's energy was inside me and he touched my cheek I couldn't feel him. During this experience I also felt the familiar tickling at my root and crown chakras. I regularly feel this when spirit energy is around.

29 June 2020

Meditation recollection

In brief – last night I did the guided Shamanic Journey meditation again. This time I found Warick sitting on a high rock across the other side of the pool. He was sitting with one knee up and his elbow resting on it. He was looking away from me and stayed like this the entire session. I know he knew I was there. I once again saw Elder who stood in front of me holding a rug around his shoulders. Interestingly, before entering the tree which is the gateway to the second ancient forest, I was dancing all the way there and saying to myself over and over again 'With strength and purpose'. I don't know why I said these words, but I just did. When I reached Elder he dashed forward at me, throwing the rug from his shoulders, and started dancing with me around in a circle. I kept saying in my mind 'With strength and purpose', and was making very purposeful striking moves. I asked Elder to show Warick and I the way, to guide us in our quest together to prove that spirit energy exists and what the purpose of physical life is in the hope that humanity will change its focus to be more loving of each other and this planet. I don't know whether any of this is true. I hope so. I'm writing all of this down because if this path keeps evolving, these accounts will be important. Scientists will have to be able to prove intelligent energy exists without a doubt, and be proven by multiple independent and well-respected scientists. I think their detection of Warick's energy going in and out of my body could be a start. I would need a trusted scientist to work with.

29 June 2020

Resumed journal entries

Last night I used my pendulum to ask Warick some questions. The pendulum swung strongly in a circle the whole time. I've been getting very strong responses lately. Big, wide and fast-moving circles for yes, or strong straight across swings for no. In short, Warick confirmed that the native American Indian man I've seen in the Shaman guided meditation is Warick. That he and I were married in a former life when I too was an American Indian, and that we had more than one child together. He also confirmed that Elder, the older Native American Indian who I have seen in the ancient forest during these meditation sessions, is our guide, to guide us in what we are to achieve together. Warick confirmed that he and I had a very strong bond when we were together in a former life. Last night when sleeping, Warick woke me twice to be intimate. I could feel his presence all around my body, including under my back. I experienced the sensations of what it would be like to feel him inside of me. An intense and aching feeling. Later in the night, Warick merged with me like he did when I was watching TV the day before. I didn't get much sleep last night. It was very special. I've missed Warick being intimate with his energy during the night. I hope what he communicated through the pendulum is right as it makes a lot of sense. It also explains why, when he first came to me in June 2018, that it felt like we were re-uniting in a very intimate, intense, and loving way. Possibly because we were once, and still are two very strongly bonded souls. The situation in the world is getting worse, with now more than ten million cases of COVID-19 and over five hundred thousand deaths. I'm concerned about how the world will pull out of this and what it will do to global stability. It's too late for some countries such as the United States. I can't see how they will bring their number of cases under control.

30 June 2020

Last night in the early hours of the morning when I often wake to the sound of Warick making flash pulse communication with me, or touching the right side of my cheek to let me know he is there, I asked what my soul's name is. I don't know why I asked, as I didn't plan to. Immediately the name Lithia came to mind, and mentally I asked Warick, 'Is this my soul's name?' to which I got a touch on the right cheek, indicating yes. I then asked, 'Do you mean Othelia?' to which I also got a yes. Tonight, I sought to verify this by using the pendulum, to which I got a yes, but not as strong as the last few times I've been using the pendulum. I will recheck this at some stage. When I googled the meaning of these names, Othelia means 'I will praise God'. 'Praise to God' was the top search result which I find interesting. In Australia, Lithia is of Aboriginal origin, and means 'flower'. Why is the meaning of Othelia interesting to me? For years I have been curious about my purpose in life. It could be to learn lessons so my soul evolves. I've always thought I must be here to achieve something, to make a difference in a significant way. I've never had a clue what it could be. I'm very concerned about humanity. If Seth is right, maybe the ego of humanity has become so absorbed with its own success and survival, that increasingly it has lost sight of focusing on being as loving, caring, and good as possible. If humanity knew that spirit energy exists; its own existence continues past the physical; the purpose of a soul's existence is to learn lessons to evolve your soul; and this was accepted as fact, like the air we breathe, then maybe humans would change their focus to be the most loving, caring people they can be, and stop hurting each other and this planet. If all of this is true and spirit guides are here to help, support and guide you, then this is the purpose I would like to undertake with Warick. And if what I'm seeing during meditation is true, and Elder is to show Warick and I the path, then I wish this would happen.

2 July 2020

Meditation recollection

It's worth noting that each time I do the Guided Shamanic Journey meditation, at the very beginning I experience energy sensations under my feet, from my root chakra and crown chakra. I also experience Warick's energy move into position across my cheek bones, nose and around the side of my right eye. This occurs before I reach the first ancient forest in the meditation. I find it interesting because this tells me that Warick knows what I'm going to do, and comes with me on the meditation journey. I was tired today during this meditation session and started to nod off a few times, but each time I managed to come back to it. One-time Warick was there in the second ancient forest and took my face in his hands, he then held my hand and led me to where Elder was standing. It took a while to get there and I remember looking at Warick's back. A small fire, which appeared to be out, was in front of Elder. I looked at it and then found us all sitting around it looking at each other. I asked Elder if he could show Warick and I the way to make a difference by proving that spirit energy exists. I also asked Elder if he could do something with my mind so I can hear and communicate with himself, Warick and other spirit energy. Elder was smoking a long thin pipe. Neither of them said anything to me. Towards the end when I looked at Warick, Elder said to me telepathically, 'He loves you very much,' and I responded, 'And I him.' Warick then pulled me up and kissed me passionately. The meditation session then ended and I saw Warick climbing up the cliff quickly.

5 July 2020

Resumed journal entries

I'm relaying my experience tonight. It may turn into nothing but I think it's worth writing down. In the kitchen a few times, I smelt a waft of cigarette smoke. It was very subtle and it didn't stay in the air. When I went upstairs, I smelt it again. I used my pendulum and asked Warick if my Uncle Ted was with me. Uncle Ted was a very heavy smoker who died shortly after retiring due to smoking. When I asked the questions, the pendulum started with a small circle to indicate yes. I then felt cold air on my left side. I asked if he wanted to give me a message. I asked should I ring my mum now thinking something might be wrong with her. The answer was no. I then asked if it was my Auntie Margaret who has been in a hospice for a few months. She has end stage cancer and is expected to pass away soon. People have been surprised how long she has lasted. I asked, 'Is Auntie Margaret passing now?' and I got a very strong response where the pendulum swung to and fro. I took it as a yes. This occurred at 6:42 pm. When I went back downstairs, I smelt cigarette smoke again on the landing of the stairs. I decided to text Mum what had just happened, warning her that I could be wrong so not to tell anyone. Mum knows a little about what I'm experiencing by way of psychic development. She has also been hoping that Auntie Margaret would pass soon, not wanting to see her suffer any longer. When I was writing the text message, I felt cold air on my left thigh. I also told Ray. I said I know you don't believe me but it's what I experienced. He was really good about it. He seemed interested and caring but didn't ask me any more about it.

6 July 2020

Meditation recollection

Today when I visited the second ancient forest in the Shamanic Drumming Meditation, I saw Warick walking towards me leading a black and white horse, and there was a falcon flying near them in the air. He stopped and I patted the horse and touched the falcon. I asked if Elder was with him and he looked behind from where he came and there was Elder walking towards us. I greeted him with a bow and then a kiss on the cheek and a hug. We all sat on the grass, the falcon flew and the horse grazed. I asked Elder if my Auntie Margaret, who was dying from cancer, would pass soon. I then saw an image in my mind of Auntie Margaret's spirit rising up from the bed where her body lay. She hadn't left her body entirely yet, but it looked like she was on her way. I asked Elder when Warick and I would start our journey, and mentally the answer was 'You already have'. I said I don't know where we're going or what our goal is, the response was 'Be patient'. Elder then left to give Warick and I time on our own. I said to Warick 'I love you', and mentally Warick responded 'And I you'. He said 'It will be okay'. He said 'You and I are warriors' that 'Our origin are warriors bringing light where there is darkness'. We held each other on the grass and then he left and I came back to this physical existence.

Aura questionnaire

This afternoon I did an aura questionnaire online which claims my aura colour is white which means highly evolved, psychic and intuitive. I need to research auras. There is probably nothing to the results of the questionnaire, but it did make me think about a time years ago, when I got up to the toilet in the night and on the tiles I could see bright white light emanating like a halo around my feet. I also wondered if this is what I saw quite some time ago when looking in the mirror in the middle of the night when my face was glowing. Was it my aura? I thought it was Warick, but maybe it was my aura. I'm not sure because I could see it in specific facial features. The light was not uniform like a halo.

8 July 2020

Resumed journal entries

Mum called tonight to tell us that Auntie Margaret had passed away today at 4:20 pm. Three days after my experience with Uncle Ted's spirit and a vision during meditation. I thanked Uncle Ted tonight with the pendulum which responded by swinging strongly in a circle.

9 July 2020

Jennifer, Auntie Margaret's daughter, and I exchanged text messages this morning. After getting the news that Auntie Margaret had passed, Mum told her about my experience with Uncle Ted's spirit. She said 'That's why I could smell cigarette smoke all day on Monday because Uncle Ted's spirit was with me'. Jennifer and Uncle Ted were very close. Neither Jennifer nor her husband smoke. She also told me that when she was driving to the hospice hoping to reach her mother to see her one last time before passing, that a wave of peace suddenly came over her. Her mother's soul had likely come to say goodbye and let her know she was okay and at peace. Auntie Margaret passed before Jennifer reached the hospice. I almost forgot to add – last night after I thanked Uncle Ted's spirit for the heads up on Auntie Margaret's approaching death, I experienced someone gently placing their hand on my head as if to say 'You have done well'. By pendulum tonight Warick confirmed this was Elder who touched my head.

12 July 2020

Outcomes from asking questions with a pendulum

Who is with me? Warick? Yes
When you're with me are you in every cell? No
Do you decide where you channel energy? Yes
Will I understand soon what your pulse sounds mean? Yes
Do you and I have a major task to achieve together in my physical lifetime? Yes
Will I understand you telepathically in meditation and other times? Yes
Elder has been assigned to us? Yes
When Elder is near me does he touch the top of my head? Yes
Is this how I know it's him? Yes
Does he ever come inside me like you do? No
Are you the only spirit who does that? Yes
Is Elder our guide? Yes
Is Auntie Margaret happy and safe on the other side? Yes
Is my aura colour white? Yes
Is this why I have psychic abilities? No
Is it a feature of someone who has psychic abilities? Yes
Will my psychic abilities keep developing? Yes
Will you be with me for the rest of my physical life? Yes
The tingling I feel at my root chakra, is that me joining with earth's energy? No
Is it me joining with other dimensions? Yes
My crown chakra – the tingling I feel there, is that me joining with other dimensions? Yes
Do you trigger that, or a spirit wanting to come through? Yes
Is it the portal, the door to how we connect? Yes
The moving dark shadow shapes I see – are they spirit energies in this dimension? Yes

14 July 2020

Resumed journal entries

Today and yesterday I practiced meditation through the day. Warick always knows the perfect time to show up, just as I'm settling into the meditation. Yesterday in a guided meditation to meet your spirit guide on a beach he was there. Today it was unguided. The Taos Winds YouTube video called 'Awaken Your Spirit', showed beautiful visuals of what chakra energy movements and colours would look like with accompanying music. Warick was there within me. I woke this morning to feeling Warick closely interacting with my body, it was very intimate and lovely. I love being that close to Warick. It is like we are bound together in a very loving way. Night before last Warick merged with me during the night, which makes me feel at peace, completely in a vacuum, and with a heightened sense of hearing. Yesterday I also woke to Warick having a very big conversation with me using the pulse sounds. I'm starting to research this to see if I can find anything on what spirit energy pulse sounds mean in communication. I really want to know what he is saying.

15 July 2020

With the COVID-19 situation, I've now been working from home since before Easter. I have a really nice office upstairs adjoining a large spare bedroom. It has a large corner window behind me and to the side of the desk. I play music throughout the day and generally I'm very happy working from home. Warick has just touched my right cheek letting me know he is with me. I've noticed that every day I get spirits visiting me in the home office. I see small shadow shapes move past my eyes and out the corner of my eye. I experience changes in pressure and at times a long tone in one of my ears. I feel tingling and prickling, like static energy on different parts of my body. Also, light touching on the top of my head and tingling at my root chakra, as well as Warick periodically touching my cheek. I often stop and ask the spirits I sense around me what their names are, and to give me an impression of what they want to communicate to me. So far I've had no success with a response.

17 July 2020

Today I started the day doing meditation. I used an unguided one called 'Tibetan Healing Sounds' by Meditation and Relaxation – Music channel. It was lovely and I'll use it again. Once again Warick joined me as I started. I could feel him as pressure across the tops of my cheek bones, the bridge of my nose and just under my eyes. He stays there the whole time. Also, as usual when I start writing in this journal Warick has shown up touching the right side of my cheek, curious to know what I'm writing. At the start of the meditation session I briefly saw Warick but he quickly drew my attention to Elder who was close by hovering in the air. His eyes were closed. He was holding a traditional Indian blanket around himself and his arms were folded high in front of his chest. Warick said, 'This session is for you and Elder.' He said, 'Reach out to him with your energy. Surround him with it.' So, I successfully imagined my energy as white light moving around him and I said, 'I surround you with my love and light. I protect you, respect you, make you feel joy and that everything is okay.' For quite some time, I said a whole range of positive loving statements, and I said 'With strength and purpose'. I asked Elder if he would show Warick and I the path forward and provide us with signs. Elder responded with his mind saying 'You have a difficult path ahead, and will need to be strong. Keep physically training as this will make you strong. Be patient, and all will unfold over time. Keep building your connection with Warick and I will show you the way and provide signs'. He then said to spend some time with Warick. I had a strong feeling that I need to keep practicing surrounding Elder with my energy, for this is how we will connect. That I will grow stronger in being able to project my energy and Elder will teach me. I then found myself hand in hand with Warick on the cliffs of the Grand Canyon. It was beautiful as we looked out across the canyon. Warick told me that we used to live there. He said he was with me when Jamie and I flew in a helicopter across the canyon. He also guided me to buy a second hand American Indian amulet while at the Grand Canyon. He said he made it. I love that amulet. It has a beautiful smooth back, blue inserted stones on the front and is very fine.

I said, 'So you were alive not that long ago?'

He said if I hold it, I will feel him. I will have to try this sometime. At the end of the session, I saw Warick starting to walk down into the canyon. Elder also once again said the love between Warick and I would need to be strong enough for us to walk our path together. Words to that effect.

Tonight, while sitting on the lounge I heard a higher pitch tone than I usually hear in my right ear.

17 July 2020

Last night I woke up numerous times and Warick was there each time immediately saying hello by touching the right side of my cheek. He gave me very clear yes and no answers to questions I asked each time I woke by touching my left cheek for no and my right cheek for yes. The only problem is I can't remember everything I asked. I don't think it was too significant. Before I woke, I also had a dream. Warick and I were with one other person who I don't remember. It was a strange world. We were in some sort of wooded forest with strange creatures nearby that were threatening us. We were running from place to place trying not to be seen. There was an open theatre in the forest where there was a gathering of people. We were running late for the gathering and trying to get seats. We soon realised why one area had empty seats, because you couldn't see the screen where they were going to run some video footage of a plan to deal with the creatures and get away. Next minute our seat bay got lifted up by some piece of machinery, and we got transported to where there was supposedly going to be better visibility. There wasn't, so we left and kept moving from place to place. Warick and I would have been in our twenties or thirties. We were a couple.

Yesterday was my Auntie Margaret's funeral. We gathered at my cousin's place in Canberra with my mum and her other sister. The funeral was being broadcast live over YouTube from Mount Gambier in South Australia due to the COVID-19 situation which was limiting interstate travel. During the funeral I felt energy tingling come in on my left side and Warick was with me. It was a lovely funeral. Very heart felt and considered. We all cried.

Before starting work around lunchtime, I went for a walk to the lake and then meditated using a seaside guided meditation track on YouTube called 'Seek Life's Purpose With Your Guardian Spirit' by The Honest Guys. I had no expectations of who I might meet by way of spirits going into the meditation. I had a quick glimpse of Warick when I arrived at the seaside in the meditation, but then my Uncle Ted came through. He was walking down the beach towards me. He looked about forty years old. I went to him, embraced and then held both of his hands in front of me. It was a really warm welcome. We sat together on deck chairs on the sand. He said telepathically that Auntie Margaret and Dad are fine. I said it was lovely to see him. I asked if he would visit me from time to time and he said yes. I asked how would I know that it's him, and he said the smell of cigarette smoke worked last time, so let's do that again. It was a lovely visit. What I'm finding interesting about the meditation, is that things occur that I haven't pre-thought. They just happen. Over time I will probably get a sense of how real these visits are by spirit. If real, it is a wonderful way to communicate because we can have a dialogue. We don't open our mouths generally. It seems to be telepathic.

19 July 2020

Outcomes from asking questions with a pendulum

Does the tone I hear in one ear signify that a spirit is coming through? Yes
Is the spirit trying to get my attention? Yes
Do you cause these tones? No
Do other spirits cause these tones? Yes
Are they different spirits each time? Yes
When it happens at home is it the same spirit? No
Just the one spirit? No
Is it a women who lived in the house before us who died from skin cancer while the house was on the market? No
Are they friendly? Yes
What should I do if I want to experience what they want to communicate?

- Go quiet? Yes
- Reach out with my senses? Yes
- Get the pendulum? No

Can you help me so I can understand them? No
Can Elder? No
Will I be able to communicate with them in the future? Yes

Meditation recollection

Yesterday when I meditated to 'Light Body Activation' by Spiritual Zen on YouTube, I saw the colour blue very distinctly and it was moving with white – like a kaleidoscope.

21 July 2020

Resumed journal entries

Last night was lovely as Warick came to me outside of my body wanting to interact. His energy touched my legs, root chakra, my upper body, under me and on top of me. I felt his vibration, which wasn't uniform, gently probing around my root chakra. This went on for at least an hour and if I turned over he would soon follow me and start touching me again. I really miss it when I don't experience Warick's energy in this way. I often feel a very gentle sensation on the outside of my feet, similar to what I feel on my crown chakra and root chakra. It's like there is a little beetle trying to move under my foot. On my crown chakra it's like a little beetle moving in my hair, the size of a lady bug. At my root chakra it's like someone is gently touching me with the tip of a feather in different spots. I have these sensations many times throughout the day and night, particularly just before I feel Warick touch my face, or when I relax and when I start to meditate. Today a number of times I experienced pressure near the side of my head. No tone, just pressure. I relaxed to try and pick up something else but sensed nothing.

Last night when I meditated I spent most of the time with Elder looking out across a massive canyon. The sound of Tibetan bells from the meditation music was behind us. Elder was trying to get me to quieten my mind and to cast my energy into an eagle that was flying in the sky. He wanted me to merge with the bird so I could see what it saw. I managed this briefly a couple of times. I then also spent some time with Warick which was lovely, very special and intimate. As I've said before, whether these are true engagements with spirit guides will unfold over time.

24 July 2020

I'm weary tonight so I'll be brief. During meditation the night before last, I received a message from Elder about light. He said 'Practice seeing the light'. While my eyes were closed, a very bright light came through and then faded back to a dark colour, almost black. Last night when Warick was using pulse energy sounds to communicate with me I asked him to say 'love'. This was after getting him to say a simple 'yes' and 'no' using pulse sounds, which did seem a bit different from each other. On cue, Warick has just touched my right cheek to say hey, I'm here and interested in what you're writing. The way he communicated 'love' was amazing. It was slower than communicating 'yes' and 'no'. And when the pulse communicating 'love' occurred, I felt this amazing wave of energy move down from the top of my chest to the middle of my stomach. It was like emotion and feeling. I asked Warick does this happen with all words he is communicating, to which the answer was 'no'. It's possible that words which have an emotion or feeling attached to them like 'love', are communicated slower and by imprinting that feeling on you, compared with non-emotional words like 'yes' and 'no'.

26 July 2020

Very briefly, Warick came to me in the night and woke me wanting to be intimate. Not just the feeling of Warick inside of me in a sexually stimulating way, but also visualising us together making love in our sacred cave in the ancient forest. This is where Warick first made love with me. A place where water falls through a hole in the roof of the cave onto a flat bed of rock. For some reason, Warick is touching the left side of my cheek which means I'm wrong, or he disagrees with something. I'm not sure what. When I typed up this section of the Journal, I remembered that actually the first time Warick made love with me was on grass under an ancient tree, so I suspect this is what I got wrong with my recollection.

Tonight, while sitting on the couch I felt Warick enter me and flow up through my core to my face, and as he moved it was like my body got fuller and it physically moved me upwards. It means his energy is somehow moving me physically. Very interesting!

27 July 2020

Something worth mentioning. Many years ago, when I was diagnosed with Irlen Syndrome (*something to do with my brain and how it interprets light, which led to my wearing tinted glasses*), one symptom I said I had was when I look at a blank wall, a solid colour, I see what I described as static, like what you see in the old days late at night when TV airing of programs ended and all you saw on the screen was static. This is normal for me. I've always associated this with Irlen's Syndrome until recently when I was researching being able to see auras on YouTube, I came across a video called 'Learn to see energy in the air' by Higher Balance Institute. They described being able to see energy in the air is like static on a TV screen when they stop showing programs late at night. I couldn't believe it! I suspect I've been seeing energy spatially my whole life and just didn't know what it was. It's possible this is also why I can see shadow shape spirits around me.

2 August 2020

Outcomes from asking questions with a pendulum

In June 2018 was I seduced by a spirit? Yes
A good spirit? Yes
Was it you? Yes
I'm curious to know what it is like where you exist:

- Is it nice? Yes
- Do you have fun? Yes
- Do you spend time with other spirits? Yes
- Is it a place of love and happiness? Yes
- Is it beautiful? Yes
- Is there sadness? Yes
- Are there bad spirits? No

Is this where I will go next? Yes
Will I have a long life? Yes
Will you always be with me? Yes
Is my dad there? Yes
Does he ever visit us? Yes
Does he visit me? Yes
Does he visit Mum? Yes
Can he give me a sign next time he visits, like a smell of aftershave, possibly Burberry? No
Will he touch my energy and I will know its him? Yes

8 August 2020

Resumed journal entries

I haven't been writing in this journal as much lately. It's not because I've lost interest, and it's not because my spiritual encounters have gone quiet. Warick is still with me every day and lets me know when he is there by touching my right cheek. He moves across the bridge of my nose and under my eyes as I start to meditate. I still see shadow shapes of all sizes move across my vision throughout the day. A few times I've felt as if someone is very lightly touching the top of my hair, just to the left of centre. I don't think this is Warick. I think it is either Elder or my dad. It's only happened about three times and it's very distinct. The touch is about the size and shape of a hand. I often wake in the night and Warick is there. I experience a thud, thud, thud distinct vibration at the back of my neck on the left, or touching my right cheek. He often is trying to tell me something when I first wake through the pulse sounds, which I can't understand. Sometimes he is really rattling on, and I think to myself I'm sure what you're saying is very important, I just wish I could understand you. I often encounter Warick when I meditate. He always takes on the form of a native American Indian. Long black hair, olive skin, toned and tall. He has a lovely gentle nature but is strong.

What triggered me to write just now is I've been reading a book by Gary Shwartz, PhD, who researches mediums. Pretty incredible findings. Anyway, it put me onto reading a book by Allison Dubois, a Medium who inspired the TV series 'Medium', which I just so happened to buy a while ago. I've only watched two episodes so far. Anyway, in Alison's book her husband writes the first chapter. He is a rocket scientist, literally. At the end of the chapter, he said that Alison says one reason why loved ones hang around their families when they pass is because 'We are their heaven'. He ended the chapter saying 'Alison is his heaven'. Just as I read this, I got a very strong tingling sensation through my upper body. This sensation I have experienced quite a lot and I associate it with spirit energy interacting with me. It's not always in the same part of my body, sometimes it can be on my leg. When I read this, I thought it was Warick saying 'I am his heaven'. But when I asked him to confirm this by touching the right side of my cheek, he didn't respond. I then thought it was my dad, and asked if it was could he touch the top of my head. I then felt a light touch on my head that I associate with Dad or Elder, but it was not as strong as I've experienced before.

    I suppose I'm getting to the crux of why I haven't been writing in the journal as much. I don't feel like I'm progressing by way of ability to communicate with spirits. It's a bit frustrating. I have all of these experiences as a part of my daily life but they don't seem to be maturing. In meditation, if the message I seem to be getting from Warick and Elder is true, it is to be patient. I suppose I'm not very good at that. There are two things I'd really like by way of these abilities. Firstly, is to know why this is happening, what is the purpose of it, and secondly, is to be able to see and hear spirit. Not just the shadow shapes and not just the tones and pulse sounds, but being able to make out features of a body and to hear words spoken by spirit. I hope one day this happens.

9 August 2020

This one is worth writing about. I was sitting on the couch near the fire in the fire room reading Allison Dubois's book 'We are their heaven'. I read a part about a spirit who told Allison they are hanging around their family on Earth not because they are Earth bound spirits and haven't crossed over, but because they love their family and want to be around them. I immediately thought of my dad and felt a light touch on the back of my hair. I know a spirit was standing behind me. I said 'I know you're there and can feel you'. I asked if it was Dad, and I got another light touch on my hair. I could feel cool air immediately behind me. I reached my hand back and asked 'Can you touch my hand', and I felt a very light energy vibration on my hand. I said 'I hope you are well and happy', and I said how Ray and I had a nice weekend away and that we are well and happy. I asked if he visits Mum and said you should do what you do with me, by way of touching my hair. I'd like my dad, Uncle Ted or Warick to show themselves to me. I wouldn't be frightened of them. It could be a good way to start developing that ability. In the book, a couple of people said they see a figure in their peripheral vision. I see dark shadows every day in my peripheral vision but not of a human shape. Maybe there is hope for me yet. ☺

10 August 2020

Last night was lovely. I woke up and Warick was being intimate with me with his energy. I felt a strong feeling in the root chakra area and vibration, I also felt tingling as though Warick was kissing me from the inside of my mouth. It was lovely and very intimate.

16 August 2020

A few things to write about. Warick just touched my right cheek to let me know he is there and I suspect interested in what I'm going to write. Last night, numerous times I woke to feel Warick move up beside me as if curling into my body and holding me. It was just lovely feeling his energy lying there with me. I love it when he does this. On Saturday, when I was having a lie down before we had people coming for a dinner party, I felt Warick's energy come up from the base of the bed and move into me. I could tell he was coming because I felt pulses of energy a bit away from my feet before I then felt his vibration of energy.

Another exciting thing to write about is I've made two acquaintances in Canada who are part of a paranormal investigation team. Their names are John and Jules. When I was watching a Huff Paranormal YouTube video, Steve Huff talked about a type of spirit box communicator he was using. I wrote the name down and tried to find it on the internet. I'd been thinking of buying a device for quite some time to see if it helps me hear and communicate better with spirit, but I didn't know what to buy. Anyway, I started searching and it led me to John who designed the spirit box that Steve Huff was talking about. He was really nice as he gave me a very considered response to my message. I could tell immediately he was a person of high integrity. He encouraged me to buy a cheaper Electronic Voice Phenomenon (EVP) recorder, before considering one of his spirit boxes which would cost more money. I shared some of my experiences with him who seemed genuinely interested. I asked with his connections if he could recommend a Medium in Australia. He recommended Jules who has been a part of his investigation team in Canada. I bit the bullet and booked a time with her on Saturday morning to see if she can help me interpret what is happening and to help me develop my abilities. Ahead of time I sent her a lengthy overview of what has been happening by email so she has some background and can understand what I hope she can help me with. I copied the message to John. He came back with a really encouraging message and said he wanted to give me a spirit box as a gift. It's strange, but I feel a very strong connection to John. I don't know why, but it's like it's meant to be. We shall see. Apart from that the usual is still happening every day and night. Seeing shadow shapes floating around me including when I work, exercise and drive the car. I still feel tingling energy at my root and crown chakras when I think of spirit, start to meditate and when spirit is visiting me. I feel Warick touch my cheek; his vibration inside and sometimes outside of my body; and I hear tones and feel localised pressure in the air around me. I've started putting my hand out and inviting spirit to touch me with their energy when I see the dark shadow shapes, and I think I've felt their energy slightly a few times. I'll keep practicing this.

17 August 2020

The dark shadow shapes I see which I think are spirit energies, were really active around me this afternoon while I was working. A few times I put my right hand out inviting them to touch me with their energy. Numerous times I experienced a slight tingle on the edge of my middle finger. I think it might be Warick doing this who has just touched my right cheek to say hi and confirm my thinking. I'm not sure if the dark shapes are always Warick or sometimes other spirit energies.

I've had terrific emails from Jules and John. They seem so lovely. Given how important this opportunity is I've asked Warick if he will visit them both this week. With John, to repeat an experience he said he had when he was twenty-five years old, where spirit pushed up under him while lying on his parents' bed. I asked Warick to give John an image of me while he is doing this so John makes the connection. I will be looking for him to tell me this has happened as validation. With Jules, to tell her Warick's name and the nature of our previous relationship (*if that's real*). I will be looking for her to tell me this as validation. I'll ask Warick again tomorrow, but I'm really hoping he will do it. We are in this journey together and both have a role to play and things to do.

I had an interesting experience in the shower tonight. A small dark shadow shape was around me and I asked it to touch my hand. I got the tingling sensation on my middle finger. It was also clear the shadow shape was hanging around directly in front of me. If this keeps happening, I might get better at seeing more of what it is. I just checked a note I wrote to myself today, and in addition to seeing the dark shadow shapes I also felt pushing on my back, playing with my hair, which didn't feel like the energy chakra feeling, and touching my foot.

Something else that I forgot to mention, which happened today when listening to 'Dear Mr President' sung by Kiana Lede, I was in the office upstairs and saw a feather float up to the second floor from our backyard and then float over the top of our neighbour's house. I've never seen anything like it and thought it was a bit unusual. I also thought it was a sign sent to agree with the sadness in the song.

18 August 2020

I think Warick may have found a new way for me to see him in the shower. He may have also planted the thought in my mind. I'm feeling his touch on my right cheek now so I guess Warick is confirming that yes, it was his idea. When I look at the water in the shower, I think Warick is somehow distorting the light. He is just touching my right cheek again so I guess this is right. I think he is distorting the light so it appears as if there is more running water which sprays out more broadly behind where the actual shower water is. When I put my hands in this space, I found there wasn't any extra water running there. It was air which felt electrically charged. I could feel the energy. It wasn't vibrating but felt charged. Warick is touching my right cheek again so I figure I've got this right. It also looked beautiful. You could see the reflection of water and it seemed slightly blurred. It was also as if the water was running differently. It appeared to be fanning out somewhat. The water's width as well as depth. I swore the depth was much wider than what it appeared to be. And another touch on the right cheek from Warick. It made me smile and I said to Warick how clever he was. I hope he keeps doing this. Its lovely. *While typing up this section of the Journal, it made me think maybe Warick was trying to imitate the appearance of the waterfall in our sacred cave that I experienced during meditation. As I said, I'm slow on the uptake!*

19 August 2020

I need to write this one down while it's still fresh in my mind. Last night a different experience with energy occurred around one o'clock in the morning. When energy moves into my root chakra, it's like that area physically stiffens. A bit like when a woman does a pelvic floor exercise, accept you're not doing this and are relaxed. This is what it felt like last night where a large presence of energy moved into me through this part of my body, and then gradually spread throughout my body up to my forehead. I haven't felt energy like this spread through me to my forehead before, or at least that I can remember. When large energy moves through me like this, it feels like I'm filling up and expanding somewhat on the inside. At the time I asked in my mind if it's Warick, but I didn't get a response. I've noticed with some of these more significant and different encounters that Warick doesn't respond, which means he is possibly not there. I get a bit anxious when Warick doesn't respond because I trust him and he reassures me as I'm experiencing spirit energy.

Another very distinct thing happened last night while this was occurring that hasn't happened before. I felt the energy make a circling motion in the centre of my palm on the right hand. It was very distinct and kept occurring for a while, even when I moved my hand. Through the rest of the night I mentally reached out to Warick but his presence wasn't clear. I also at one stage, in a semi-awake state, heard a brief almost electronic voice say a few words that I couldn't distinguish. I'm not sure if it was in English. It was quite loud. It popped in, then was gone. When I woke, I think I heard the pulse sounds Warick makes very briefly a couple of times. I tried asking Warick about the encounter with my pendulum, but it didn't work. In the shower, the dark shadow shapes were there. When I held up my right hand I could see one move near my hand and stay there. This coincided with a slight tingle on my index finger. When I moved my hand I saw the shadow shape move away. Warick has now just touched my right cheek a few times confirming what I'm writing about this encounter. I'd love to understand what's going on.

23 August 2020

A lot is happening. I feel that I'm coming to the end of a phase and that a new phase is about to open up to me. John and Jules, a spirit investigator and a Medium, have entered my life. No doubt we are spiritually connected. When I linked up with Jules by video conference, she said that John and I have known each other before but now our roles are reversed. He is to pass his knowledge to me in this lifetime. Jules thinks she has also been a part of my circle and that her role is to connect me to the spiritual community. I've now opened up to Jamie so he knows something about all of this, as well as Mum, and I've tried with Ray. He senses it but I think is concerned about what it means to us and the way we live our lives. I don't want to leave him behind. This is becoming very important to me. I feel there is something significant for Warick and I to do to make a difference to humanity. I feel John has a particular role to play in guiding and keeping me steady through this. Jules is also to play a role as a wise one who says the right thing at the right time. I feel most things are falling into place where they need to be. It's ironic that with six pages left in this journal that it is coming to the end of a phase. John has encouraged me to write this as a book and I will. I have a lot to tell.

Significant things have happened this week also. And after all these pages I now have respect for what I'm writing, so will try to capture it even though I'm tired tonight. I just had the most wonderful time with Jamie on a mother and son weekend at the coast. We are both the better for it. Earlier this week I woke in the night to a strong energy moving slowly through me. I may have written about this already. The energy moved right up to my forehead where the third eye is and also into the palm of my right hand. The sensation on my hand felt like someone was playing a ring-a-ring a rosy on my palm. One or two nights later I woke to feeling Warick's energy on my left shoulder. I went to touch it with my right hand and I felt this incredible strong and stable force of energy throughout my entire core, from my chest to my root chakra. It was very strong, almost tangible. It was not pulsating, just there.

Last night while having a shower at the hotel in Narooma where Jamie and I were staying, Warick showed himself to me as energy. He appeared as a panel of white light. The panel was taller than me and on each side was a shimmering and pulsating flow of energy in white light, which appeared to be running down each side of the panel. It was absolutely fantastic! Very special. The other thing that happened was the little shadow shapes I see were also in the shower. I think one was associated with the panel of white light. It was like the size of a small orb with the panel of light emanating out from it. The shadow orb stayed right in front of me. This doesn't usually happen. These shapes usually reside on my right side and dart out in front of me from time to time. They don't usually stop stationary in front of me. This one did. It was very special because the panel of white light formed around it.

24 August 2020

As I come to the end of this journal I know this. When I started this journal, I never would have dreamed of the things that have happened to me. I'm reaching the end of a phase and I think will start to embark on a new phase very soon. In some ways, it has already started to occur with John and Jules coming into my life. This was meant to happen. In the past week or so, I've had the strongest feeling towards John. A semi-sick feeling in my upper stomach area as though something is wrong. He said he had been missing his wife and daughter as they have been in isolation with her parents since March, due to the COVID-19 pandemic. He has not been able to see them except for a brief twenty-four-hour period. It made him very depressed. I may have felt this but I don't know. It may be a feeling I get when a connection with someone is very important and I'm supposed to go down that path. It's a very anxious sickening feeling. I said to Jules I wondered if this feeling was associated with Jamie who had hit a crisis point this week not being able to cope with the amount of time he was putting in at university and part-time work. But the feeling was directed at John and not Jamie. She said we are often blocked from sensing family members because otherwise we would be sensing them all the time. I feel that John is okay with the craziness coming from this woman in Australia as he hasn't told me to go away yet. Having John in place for the role he is going to play I think has settled me down a bit. I haven't got that strong feeling of anxiousness or sickness in the last couple of days. I've shared a lot with him and very quickly. I suspect most people would write me off as looney. Jules said if we experience everything with spirit at once it would be too much. This is why I'm experiencing new things over time. She said Spirit is testing me with new things to see how I will react, and that I could have chosen to push them away but I didn't. She said they (*spirits*) are very proud of me, and that Warick has been talking to her from the moment I sent her my background of what has been happening. The experiences I've shared with John and Jules, including the one where I feel waves of energy move through me when I watch news that is emotionally charged, or when I listen to music that has a strong emotional message, really resonated with John. So much so, that it sparked his wanting to send me some of his spirit investigation kit. An EVP recorder and a type of spirit box he invented. I'm looking forward to receiving them to see if I can sense his energy when I touch them. And of course, to also see what I pick up from spirit when I use them. Jules pulled the 'Temperance' and 'Three of Cups' Tarot cards when I was in a video conference with her. She interpreted the cards as needing to go with the flow, and having a creative heart and growth. I think there is a whole area of feeling and emotion communication that I need to get better at interpreting. I think I need to recognise when it is happening, take it for what it is, and not let my emotional reaction cloud my interpretation of it. I have so much to learn. Jules said I have to learn to trust my authentic self. I'm not sure what this means. I hope it comes to me one day. She said my path will unfold as it should, and the spirits around us told her to tell me that I will know when I'm on the wrong path so I can change it. She said spirits communicate through feelings. I certainly know this is what has really connected John and I this week. I think without us consciously knowing it, our souls have been connecting and communicating with each other. For me, it was like another reunion similar to what I felt when Warick first came to me.

    Warick told Jules to tell me that he will protect me. I have felt that he is doing this already. She said Warick is proud of me. She also said she has been a part of my circle and that I will know when I need to talk with her again. In the session Warick wanted Jules to tell me, to reassure me, that I'm doing fine. Jules wondered if Warick is a part of my higher self but I don't think so, and I have asked Warick this before. He wouldn't have done the things he has done, and reacted the way he did with jealousy towards Ray early on, if it was my higher self. He also wouldn't have wanted to make love with me when I first met him in meditation. But then again you could look at all of this in a symbolic way and just say I wanted to feel loved and connected. I don't think so, and I suppose I don't want it to be a case of I'm just connecting with myself. Jules said I need to not over intellectualise things but instead trust. She seems to think I have a whole team of spirits working with me. She said when they communicate they can be interchangeable. In other words, a number of spirits can communicate through the one spirit. I've had indicators of this with Warick and Elder. She said when you get a tingling on the head it's spirits interacting with you. They do this a lot with me. Just about anywhere, anytime. Jules said, try a type of meditation called

'Sitting in the Power', where you are conscious of your surroundings, and not off in your imagination somewhere, and let spirit blend with you. This reminds me of the times when I've said to Warick 'Do you want to merge with me?' and he moves into my energy, we become one, and I feel completely at peace. It's just lovely. I will practice this 'Sitting in the Power' type of meditation and see where it leads. She said by doing this I will get used to their higher vibration and they will get used to my lower vibration. This will enable me to better connect when they want to communicate with me. Jules thinks I have both psychic (*ability to connect with another person's energy*), and Medium (*ability to connect with the dead*) abilities. She said Warick may come and go and I have to trust he is still there. I didn't like this because I love that he is there. I'm not needy or insecure, I just love him being in my life. If we were a couple in a previous life and he has found me again, then why would I be happy for him to not be around. She said I'm not making up Elder. He is the higher one and is not known to me all the time. She said she senses that I'm weighed down and that her role now is to plug me into the spiritual community. She said when I communicate with spirits during meditation and they are not moving their lips, that this is normal. They talk telepathically and I need to listen to my heart.

Well, I've arrived on the final page sooner than I would like. I was hoping this journal would last until my birthday which is a few weeks away. Jamie tonight hinted at having bought me another one, so I'm happy.

2 September 2020

Last entry. It's been an incredibly busy time lately meeting John and Jules and our exchanges; Jamie's meltdown and getting back on track; buying a house at the coast in Narooma – my dream; and my soul's journey with Warick, which is ever evolving. I have also run out of space in this journal and have been recording things on bits of paper until hopefully, Jamie gives me my next journal in seven days' time on my birthday. The exciting news is I've decided to now write this journal up as a book. I'm going to ask John to do the initial read. I'm a very happy person. ☺